Good Practice Guide: **Employment**

# Good Practice Guide:
# Employment

**Brian Gegg**, Kennedys Solicitors
**David Sharp**, Workplace Law Group

RIBA ⁂ **Publishing**

© Brian Gegg of Kennedys and David Sharp of Workplace Law Group, 2006
Published by RIBA Publishing, 15 Bonhill Street, London EC2P 2EA

ISBN 1 85946 182 4

Stock Code 55694

British Library Cataloguing in Publications Data
A catalogue record for this book is available from the British Library.

Publisher: Steven Cross
Commissioning Editor: John Elkington
Project Editor: Anna Walters
Editor: Alasdair Deas
Designed and typeset by Ben Millbank
Printed and bound by Hobbs the Printer, Hampshire

# Series foreword

The *Good Practice Guide* series has been specifically developed to provide architects, and other construction professionals, with practical advice and guidance on a range of topics that affect them, and the management of their business, on a day-to-day basis.

All of the guides in the series are written in an easy-to-read, straightforward style. The guides are not meant to be definitive texts on the particular subject in question, but each guide will be the reader's first point of reference, offering them a quick overview of the key points and then provide them with a 'route map' for finding further, more detailed information. Where appropriate, checklists, tables, diagrams and case studies will be included to aid ease-of-use.

## Good Practice Guide: Employment

The most valuable asset of any business is its workforce. This excellent guide is a welcome reminder that we, as professionals, should run our practices in a businesslike and civilised manner to achieve the highest performance. This is not to say that innovation, collaboration, and creative endeavours have to cease, but only that relying on poor employment practice to achieve them has no place in a forward thinking profession.

Sustaining the profession relies on us all paying attention to employees and employment issues with the same rigour we apply to the rest of our activities.

**Jack Pringle**
*President, RIBA*

# Foreword

This is an essential guide for every office library. We often take for granted the hard work and dedication of our staff until problems arise. Without adequate attention to and support for better employment conditions and opportunities, we will continue to lose talented individuals from our offices. At a time of massive public investment in our building stock in all sectors, and a successful Olympic bid, the profession and the RIBA need to hang on to and promote the best and the most diverse range of architectural talent. The RIBA has historically avoided advising members and member practices about their legal obligations and practice management, but the time has come to step in.

The RIBA-funded research 'Why Women Leave Architecture', instigated by the RIBA Equality Forum 'Architects for Change' and carried out by the University of the West of England, pointed the finger squarely at working conditions in practices, rather than the male-dominated construction industry that has been blamed in the past. The key issues of poor pay and long hours that particularly affect women are ones that affect us all.

Of course, most of us enjoy what we do, are dedicated to our profession and put up with the long hours. This is not to say that we should expect the same of every member of our office. We are perpetuating the myth that the long-hours culture is the only way to achieve excellence. RIBA member practices should be able to operate within the law, or even better than the law prescribes, but there are too many stories of discrimination, high staff turnover and stress-related illnesses to agree that this is the reality. An improvement in working conditions will help every employee, as well as producing benefits for employers.

This guide is intended to support and direct practices, particularly those starting up or which are too small to employ human resources managers. The area of employment legislation is huge and ever changing. This guide will point you in the right direction but it is up to you, as employer or employee, to ensure that you are getting it right. The penalties for failure can be severe, but the rewards for following, or even improving on, the legislation are a sustained and dedicated workforce, the backbone of your success as a practice. Be flexible and innovative, listen, and share what works with the RIBA!

**Helen Taylor RIBA**
*Chair, Employment Task Group*

# Preface

This guide has been written to help architects understand their legal responsibilities from their perspective as employers.

The employment relationship is a complex one, particularly so for practising architects, who are likely to have working relationships with a number of parties, including full- and part-time employees, contractors, sub-contractors, consultants and fellow professional advisors. It is important that architects understand the duties they owe to these groups under employment and health and safety legislation.

In such a complex area, the scope of this guide is inevitably limited. Section 1 sets out the way in which the guide is designed to be used. It is not a comprehensive text on employment law or health and safety, and cannot be used as such; rather it is intended as a guide for architects' practices to highlight potential issues and pitfalls that arise from employment law and the related liabilities that fall on employers of all sizes.

While general principles of employment remain fairly constant, the law itself, of course, changes frequently! This guide deals with current legislation as at 31 August 2005 and what is known to be in the pipeline thereafter.

Throughout the guide, sources of further information have been provided to help you track down the original legislation as well as the very latest guidance.

**Brian Gegg** and **David Sharp**
November 2005

# About the authors

**Brian Gegg** LLB(Hons) MPhil(Cantab) joined Kennedys as a Partner in the Employment Law Group in October 2002.

Brian advises on all aspects of employment law with specialisation in a variety of industries, in particular assisting with day-to-day HR management and strategy, sensitive boardroom disputes and restructuring programmes, Tribunal and High Court litigation and injunctions, as well as non-contentious contract and policy drafting and dealing with the employment aspects of commercial deals, including M & A transactions, major projects, PFI transactions and outsourcing deals with emphasis on the application of the TUPE regulations. Brian has lectured widely on employment law and is the author of the *RIBA Student Employment Contract*. He is an Online Advisor for the Workplace Law Network. He acts for a variety of professional services partnerships and companies, including architects, surveyors, accountants and management consultants.

For more information please contact:

Kennedys Solicitors
Longbow House
14–20 Chiswell Street
London
EC1Y 4TW

tel: 020 7638 3688

e-mail: b.gegg@kennedys-law.com
www.kennedys-law.com

**David Sharp** BA(Hons) Dip.M is the founder and Managing Director of the Workplace Law Group, which provides employment law and health and safety advice to UK businesses. A former editor at Croner and publisher at Financial Times Business, David has specialised in the provision of regulatory support services for 15 years.

The Workplace Law Group provides advice and information to more than 40,000 managers through its book publishing, training and consulting, and online advice network. Its flagship print publication, *Workplace Law Magazine*, was highly commended in the PPA Magazine of the Year Awards 2005, and the company was given recognition by Jobcentre Plus for its positive approach to work with disabled people.

Workplace Law is a partner of the RIBA, providing employment advice at discounted rates to members of the Institute by telephone and through its weekly e-mail bulletin service.

For more information, please contact:
Workplace Law Group
Second Floor, Daedalus House
Station Road
Cambridge
 CB1 2RE

tel: 0870 777 8881

e-mail: info@workplacelaw.net
www.workplacelaw.net/riba

# Acknowledgements

The authors would like to thank everyone involved in helping to bring this project together, in particular: Helen Taylor, Chair of the Employment Task Group at the RIBA; other Task Group members, including Virginia Newman, Vicki Fruish, and everyone kind enough to comment on the manuscript; Richard Brindley, Brendan O'Connor and Corinne Rose in the Practice Department at the RIBA; Ciaron Dunne, for his original idea; and Helen Abbott, formerly of Workplace Law Group, for her contribution to Section 11, *Staff development*.

# Contents

# Section 1
# Employment law: the issues for architects' practices and introduction to using this guide

A key asset to any architect's business is its staff; people who service clients' needs and who provide the lifeblood and character of the firm. However, employees have a number of characteristics that represent both potential problems and benefits to a practice; in turn, these are affected by the wealth of employment law legislation operating in the UK.

- Employees are individuals, and often self-motivated professionals.
- Despite being individuals they need to operate in teams, which must work together effectively for the firm to be successful.
- Mostly they are highly skilled.
- They are human beings; not machines. As such, dealing with them effectively demands a balance of due process and psychology.
- They have rights – whether they know it or not – which flow from a number of different sources, including:

  - contractual terms of employment
  - implied terms
  - rights imposed by statute, such as the right to be paid a minimum wage and protection against unfair dismissal and discrimination
  - rights which have become commonplace through custom and practice, either in their employers' practices or within the architecture industry generally

- the broad network of employment rights arising from European law and UK law.
- They are affected by and have influence over the morale of the firm.

Employment legislation in the United Kingdom is full of pitfalls for the unwary employer. The law is constantly changing through the impact of ever-evolving regulations and the effect of case law adapting the interpretation of statutory provisions. The law provides employees with significant enforceable rights against employers. However, the converse is also true. If employment rights are properly recognised and adhered to by employers, business operations can be enhanced and morale improved.

**Using this guide**

This guide outlines the risks imposed on architects' practices by employment laws. It is not designed as a comprehensive text on employment legislation. Rather, it aims to provide managers within architects' firms with practical advice on how to identify issues or occurrences that should cause 'alarm bells' to ring, so alerting employers to the existence of an employment law risk.

Each section of this guide is split into distinct parts, as follows:

- **Issues and alarm bells**: a summary of the key issues that may affect practices and the alarm bells to be aware of.
- **Checklist**: a list of points and steps to consider when addressing issues and risks.
- **Where to look**: a list of sources of information for further details, advice or precedents.
- **Case study**: some sections include a worked example describing scenarios relevant to an architectural practice.

The sections are organised so as to mirror the chronological life of the employment relationship, from interview and selection through to retirement. As such, the guide is constructed to provide architects' firms with a first point of reference through which to identify and plan a strategy in relation to risks imposed on firms by employment law provisions.

**Employment law in context**

Even a glance at the index to this guide will demonstrate the extent to which employment law and human resources considerations govern the life of a working relationship. The topics covered reflect the rights of employees and employers (for example, contractual terms, discrimination laws, family-friendly issues, providing a safe working environment, protection of the employer's business and confidential information, and using employment policies). These rights and duties are predominately enforced in employment tribunals, although some claims can be brought in county courts or in the High Court; employment disputes and resolution are dealt with in Section 13.

The RIBA has produced the *RIBA Employment Policy* to advise employers on best practice in dealing with staff.

Notwithstanding the legal aspects highlighted by this guide, there are great benefits to be derived by companies who are perceived to be 'good employers'; in particular those who provide personal support and facilities that create enhanced loyalty, which in turn gets the best out of staff. In this guide, a number of suggestions are set out which might fall into this category. Not all items have a physical cost; many have intangible benefits, but their provision denotes a thoughtful employer.

# Section 2
# Employment status: employee or contractor?

*This section deals with the difficult but key issue of whether an individual is an employee or is really a self-employed contractor. The distinction is crucial to the question of engaging staff, the subsequent relationship and termination, because different rights and benefits attach to these two groups of workers.*

**Issues and alarm bells**

### Status

Employees and self-employed contractors have different rights. In particular, self-employed contractors have no statutory employment rights and are responsible for their own tax affairs.

The true status of an individual is ultimately a matter for a court to decide. The courts balance factors typically indicating employment status against those typically indicating self-employed status. Ultimately, the key is whether the person is an integral part of an employer company or is in business on their own account.

The construction of the contract between the individual and the company is a good place to start and set out the intentions of the parties as to the status of the individual, but it is certainly not conclusive.

Key factors to consider include the following:

- 'Control' – who really controls the individual's actions? The greater the level of control imposed on the individual, the more employee status is likely.
- Financial risk – a contractor takes more financial risk on him or herself than an employee.
- Mutuality of obligations – where an employer is obliged to provide work to an individual if it is available and the individual is obliged to take the work if it is

offered, employment status is more likely. This is often a key issue in assessing the status of casual staff contracts.

- Tax – although not determinative in itself, if Schedule E tax is paid at source by a company, the individual is more likely to be an employee.
- Labels – the fact that a contract states the status of an individual is not conclusive in law, but it can be a factor to consider in terms of the intention of the parties.
- Personal service – this is a key issue. True employees are obliged to perform tasks personally. Truly self-employed contractors can engage substitutes or delegate to them, and are usually allowed to work for other companies during any contract (employees are usually not).
- Clients – in general terms, self-employed contractors will work for more than one 'client' company. If an individual works for only one company, that will be an indicator of employment status.
- Terms and benefits – the existence of the usual 'employee' type of benefits will suggest employee status, as will provision of tools and equipment by the employer.
- Place of work – if an individual works out of his or her own offices or business premises, this will be a factor tending to suggest self-employed status.
- Conduct – it should also be noted that contracts can be implied by conduct; individuals who are not employees when they start can become employees over time.

### Workers

'Workers' are a hybrid type of staff, somewhere in between the true employee and the truly self-employed contractor. Workers benefit from various statutory rights, such as holidays under the Working Time Regulations (see Section 8), minimum wage rights (see Section 4) and discrimination rights (see Sections 5 and 6).

Truly self-employed contractors are not workers. Most statutory definitions of a worker point to individuals who work under a contract to provide services personally.

### Agencies and temps/casuals

The true status of agency-supplied staff will depend on individual circumstances. Do not assume they are always employees of the agency.

It is possible that individuals placed with a company are not actually employees of either the agency or the company. However, individuals supplied by an 'employment agency' (which seeks out candidates for permanent placement) are more likely to be clear employees of the company. Even agency temps (usually supplied by 'employment businesses', which hold a bank of agency staff to be placed temporarily) can be employees of the company, particularly if a sufficient degree of control is exercised over them.

Since the Conduct of Employment Agency and Employment Business Regulations 2003, employment agencies and employment businesses have been regulated. They are required to give more written clarity as to employment status, particularly in that an employment business must state to the individual who will pay them and whether they are employees or contractors of the employment business.

**Checklist**

- ☐ **Draft clear employment contracts or contractor contracts.**

- ☐ **To a certain extent companies can choose to structure relationships as much as possible to create employment or contractor status. The structure of proper employment contracts or contractor contracts can help.**

- ☐ **Do not make assumptions as to self-employed status; anticipate the risk of a person actually being a worker or an employee, or the risk of them bringing a claim that they have such status.**

- ☐ **Review relationships periodically, particularly long-term relationships. Remember that they may have turned into employment situations by conduct (see the risks above of implied employment status).**

- ☐ **Be able to justify any internal decisions as to whether people are employed or not. Keep records of your rationale; you may need evidence if HM Revenue and Customs queries your practices.**

- ☐ **On a practical level, it is worth remembering that employees may have more loyalty to the business and have greater long-term commitment than would self-employed contractors providing services.**

**Where to look**

**Key legislation**

Conduct of Employment Agencies and Employment Businesses Regulations 2003

Disability Discrimination Acts 1995 and 2005
Employment Act 2002
Employment Equality (Religion or Belief) Regulations 2003
Employment Equality (Sexual Orientation) Regulations 2003
Employment Relations Act 2004
Employment Rights Act 1996
Fixed-Term Employees (Prevention of Less Favourable Treatment) Regulations 2002
National Minimum Wage Act 1998
Part-Time Workers (Prevention of Less Favourable Treatment) Regulations 2000
Public Interest Disclosure Act 1998
Race Relations Act 1976
Sex Discrimination Act 1957
Social Security Contributions and Benefits Act 1992
Transfer of Undertaking (Protection of Employment) Regulations 1981
Working Time Regulations 1998

**Guidance**

### Department of Trade and Industry (DTI)

*Guidance on the Conduct of Employment Agencies and Employment Businesses Regulations 2003*
*The Employment Status of Individuals in Non-standard Employment*
www.dti.gov.uk

### HM Revenue and Customs (HMRC)

See the *Employment Status Manual* (ESM) at the HMRC website
www.hmrc.gov.uk

---

**CASE STUDY**

**Facts**

Mr Worker has been providing drawing services to Architect & Partners for the past two years. His workflow has been fairly consistent, and on many occasions he has a desk in the office and uses the firm's equipment. Many clients think he is an employee of the firm. The firm thinks he is a contractor, and pays him gross on the production of invoices. However, there is no written agreement.

CONTINUED ▶

**CASE STUDY (CONTINUED)**

Following a difference of opinion between Mr Worker and the senior partner of the firm as to the quality of some drawings he produced, the firm decides to terminate the relationship. Mr Worker immediately brings an employment tribunal claim, stating that he is an employee of the firm and claiming notice pay, holiday pay and unfair dismissal.

The tribunal weighs up the factors that point to employee status (including use of equipment, the fact that he worked almost full time for the firm and that he had no separate offices) and those pointing to self-employed status (including the fact that tax was not deducted at source and payment was on invoices, and that the firm did not have day-to-day control over his activities). Ultimately, the tribunal decides that the reality of the situation was that if work was available for Mr Worker he was not obliged to take it and the firm was not obliged to give it to him. As such there was no 'mutuality of obligation', and on that basis he was not an employee and his claims failed.

### Issues

- In this case, the employment tribunal was very close to finding Mr Worker was an employee.
- The lack of a written agreement was damaging to the firm in this situation. Although it would not have been conclusive in itself, it could have clearly set out the intentions of the parties and reflected the reality of the position at the time the relationship commenced.
- Whether 'mutuality of obligation' exists or not is always a key factor in these issues and should be considered at the start of any relationship.

# Section 3
# Recruitment and selection

*This section outlines the reasons for recruitment of staff and the benefits of effective recruitment. It also highlights the pitfalls inherent in failing to consider and implement proper procedures for selecting applicants for jobs.*

## Issues and alarm bells

Recruitment is an important issue in addressing both the current needs of a company and its future plans. The need for skills in the future has significant implications for recruitment. Effective recruitment is vital to the success and growth of any organisation; it is important to find staff with the necessary skill, expertise, qualifications and ability. Getting it wrong can be expensive.

In each case, does the firm really need to recruit a direct replacement for staff members who leave? Is internal recruitment possible? Could a job share be put in place? Would it be more cost effective to consider contractors or agency staff?

## Job descriptions

Job descriptions can help to define roles in companies. However, they can cause problems if they are too brief or too detailed. The RIBA is considering producing model job descriptions for architects.

Failure to implement and update job descriptions or job specifications can lead to problems. It can leave a firm exposed if faced with allegations of discrimination arising from a failure to select a candidate, or lead to disputes with successful candidates as to the scope of a role. For example, recruiting direct from architectural school students could lead to problems if other candidates allege that their non-selection was for discriminatory reasons.

Failure to consider and draft a proper specification for the job can lead to a lack of evidential support for the firm's view as to the type of person and skills necessary to perform the potential role.

Advertisements need particular care because they constitute statements and representations made by the company and can contain promises which become terms and conditions of employment. Remember also that promises made in interviews can become terms of employment, and that candidates have a right to see interview notes and related papers under the Data Protection Act 1998.

### Discrimination claims

There is considerable risk of discrimination claims being brought against firms by unsuccessful applicants for jobs (see Sections 5 and 6). Key areas in which issues arise concern the criteria set for jobs: advertisement wording, interviewers acting or questioning in a discriminatory manner, and unfair selection processes.

Irrational shortlisting and rejection of applicants at the shortlisting stage without proper matching against job descriptions, job specifications and criteria can lead to discrimination claims. Damages for discrimination are unlimited and can be significant. To counter discrimination claims, it is usually necessary to be able to prove (with records) that actions taken were not by reason of sex, race, disability, etc.

Managers who shortlist or interview potential applicants and make subjective judgments on criteria that are not job-related run significant risk of discrimination claims. Failure to conduct interviews in the same way with similar questions for all candidates and failure to keep records of interviews can also lead to discrimination claims.

### Immigration

Ensure that all candidates have appropriate work permits and permissions to work in the UK. Firms will commit an offence if they employ staff who are not permitted to work in the UK/EU. Requests should be made for information (such as passports) as permitted under Section 8 of the Asylum and Immigration Act 1996, but the same information must be requested from all candidates to avoid race discrimination allegations. However, it is possible to make offers that are conditional on the candidate providing proof of ability to work in the UK.

**Checklist**

☐ Consider business requirements carefully before starting a recruitment process.

☐ Draft job descriptions to provide guidance, consistency and objectivity in the recruitment process.

☐ Draft job descriptions to give a reasonable idea of what a particular job involves. Do not list every potential task or work item, instead outline main duties and responsibilities.

☐ Draft job specifications to describe the type of person required and desired skills and interests, including essential or desirable experience, qualifications, knowledge, skills and personal qualities.

☐ In advertisements, state in clear language:

- the job requirements
- criteria for the role
- a description of the firm
- the place of work
- the remuneration
- perceived duration of the role (fixed-term contract?)
- how to apply for the job.

☐ Avoid any language or requirement in advertisements that directly or indirectly discriminates against any potential application on grounds of sex, race, disability, religion or similar philosophical belief or sexual orientation (see Sections 5 and 6).

☐ Ensure that those who shortlist candidates can prove they have compared applicants to clear job descriptions, specifications and criteria, and that they do not shortlist by making assumptions.

☐ Ensure those involved in the interview and selection process are trained on employment law, equal opportunities and discrimination risks.

☐ Base selection processes on:

- the skills and abilities required to perform the role

- whether the candidate will contribute to the firm
- whether the candidate has development potential.

☐ Interviewers should prepare questions for candidates in advance and treat all candidates in the same way.

☐ Interviewers should not ask questions that are not based on skills and jobs requirements.

☐ For the most part, questions on marital status, parental status or pregnancy should not be asked. Questions on medical conditions and disabilities can be asked, together with questions on any reasonable adjustments that could be made to assist with disabilities.

☐ Make reasonable adjustments to the application and interview process for those known to have disabilities (see *Where to look*, below, and Section 6). For the most part, potential employers will only reasonably know about disabilities of candidates if the individual brings them to the employer's attention.

☐ Take great care not to make promises in interviews which cannot be kept or which conflict with other terms and conditions.

☐ Follow up interviews promptly and keep records of reasons for rejecting candidates. Record reasons when rejecting candidates. Always consider what proof or rationale will be needed if an unsuccessful applicant brings a discrimination claim.

☐ Keep a proper paper trail of advertisements, job descriptions and interview records so as to be able to prove actions and motives.

☐ Request the permitted information pursuant to Section 8 of the Asylum and Immigration Act 1996. For all candidates, use offer letters that are conditional on receipt of satisfactory proof of the right to work in the UK

☐ Take references, but note the issues relating to references set out in Section 13.

☐ Do not make assumptions about candidates. For example, people returning from career breaks may in fact have a great deal of previous experience and ultimately may need less training or supervision, even if some initial training is needed (e.g. in updating computer skills). Note that the RIBA is currently developing Continuing Professional Development (CPD) courses for returners, to help experienced architects get back into practice.

## Where to look

### Key legislation

Data Protection Act 1998
Disability Discrimination Acts 1995 and 2005
Employment Act 2002
Employment Equality (Religion or Belief) Regulations 2003
Employment Equality (Sexual Orientation) Regulations 2003
Equal Pay Act 1970
Sex Discrimination Act 1975
Race Relations Act 1976
Rehabilitation of Offenders Act 1974
Religious Belief Discrimination Act 2003
Sex Discrimination Act 1973

### Guidance

### ACAS

*Employing People: handbook for small firms*
*Recruitment and Induction: advisory booklet*
*Recruitment and Selection: guide for small firms*
*Tackling Discrimination and Promoting Equality: good practice guide for employers*
www.acas.org.uk

### Chartered Institute of Personnel and Development

*The Complete Recruitment and Selection Toolkit,* Taylor and Fox, ISBN: 0852928696
*Recruiting Within the Law,* Leighton and Proctor, ISBN: 1843980053
www.cipd.co.uk

### Commission for Racial Equality

Produces good practice guides.
www.cre.gov.uk/gdpract/index.html

### Disability Rights Commission

*Policy Statement on Employment*
www.drc-gb.org

---

### CASE STUDY

#### Facts

Mr Candidate applies for a job as an architect to Architect & Partners. He responds to an advertisement placed in an industry journal which merely states the job title and qualifications required. Mr Candidate has those qualifications.

He applies by sending in his CV, which is reviewed by the senior partner. There is no job description or job specification. The senior partner rejects the CV on its face, thinking that the English is poorly worded. Mr Candidate brings an employment tribunal claim for race discrimination, claiming that the reason he was rejected was due to his race.

Mr Candidate then applies for another position with the same firm. Again there is no job description or job specification. Architect & Partners considers that it is prudent to interview Mr Candidate and does so. The senior partner interviews him, but then rejects him without giving a proper reason. Mr Candidate brings a second employment tribunal claim, this time claiming race discrimination and victimisation (on the basis that Mr Candidate has been discriminated against because he previously brought an employment tribunal claim against Architect & Partners). Mr Candidate wins both of his tribunal claims. The tribunal infers that discrimination must have been a reason for the rejections because Architect & Partners cannot demonstrate the true reasons for the rejections. A sum of £60,000 is awarded in damages for loss of earnings and injury to feelings.

#### Issues

- Clear advertisements setting out job criteria would have helped in evidence.
- Clear job descriptions and job specifications would have helped to show that the applicants were matched against sustainable criteria.
- Checklists or question sheets to show what questions were asked of all candidates in interviews and their responses would have assisted in showing the true reason for rejection.

CONTINUED ▶

---

CASE STUDY (CONTINUED)

- Training those involved in the process would have highlighted alarm bells as to potential discrimination claims.
- Second interviews can often help in such a scenario, with more than one interviewer giving their perspectives and testing the skills of the candidate, etc.

# Section 4

# Contracts of employment: terms and duties

*This section reviews the basic content of an employment contract and then expands to review some basic employment rights inherent in an employment relationship.*

**Issues and alarm bells**

A contract of employment can arise in many ways and take many forms. A mere offer and acceptance of employment is all that is needed, even if it is verbal. Offer letters can in themselves create a contract, as can e-mail correspondence.

Without a written contract, signed to signify acceptance of the terms of employment, the employer will have no certainty as to the ambit of employment terms.

Terms of employment can arise through custom and practice (i.e. by action). For example, if a company has always paid a Christmas bonus, even though it has never been written down as a contractual term it may become a term of employment.

**Minimum written particulars**

Employers must provide employees with written particulars of certain specific contractual terms as part of a 'statement of terms' or (much better) a contract of employment (Section 1 of the Employment Rights Act 1996 – ERA).

The statement must be provided no later than two months after commencement of employment. It is usual and best practice for a formal contract covering all of the basic written particulars within it to be entered into at the outset.

The statement must contain all of the following particulars:

- names of the employer and employee
- the date the particular employment commences
- the date continuous employment started (for example, employment with a

previous employer or a previous period of employment with a practice can sometimes count towards continuous employment)

- pay intervals
- normal hours of work
- holiday entitlements, including public holidays and holiday pay
- amount and frequency of pay, or method of calculating pay
- terms as to sickness or injury and sick pay
- length of notice period
- job title and description
- duration of employment
- place of work
- any collective agreements affecting or governing employment
- if the employee is required to work outside the UK, the length of that period of work, the currency of pay and any additional pay resulting from work abroad
- whether or not there is a contracting-out certificate in force for the purposes of the Pensions Schemes Act 1993
- disciplinary rules (all employers irrespective of their size must specify any disciplinary rules applicable to the employee or refer to an accessible document containing information about disciplinary rules, and also details of a person to whom the employee can apply for the purposes of bringing any grievance).

An employment tribunal can award two to four weeks' pay per employee as a penalty for failure to provide written particulars.

### Express contract terms

Contracts of employment providing additional protection above the minimum requirements increase certainty and control and reduce risk. The checklist (below) lists some suitable additional contact clauses.

### Implied contract terms

Certain terms are implied into the employment relationship in any event, even though they are not written down.

Implied terms imposed on the employer are:

- to treat the employee with trust and confidence (including operating express terms of the contract reasonably)

- to care for employee's health and safety
- to agree a reasonable period of notice if one has not been agreed.

Implied terms imposed on the employee are:

- to treat the employer with trust and good faith
- to obey reasonable instructions
- to work with due diligence and care
- various implied duties not to disclose or use trade secrets.

### Employment benefits

The benefits provided by employers to their employees will often vary according to the company's preferences and the employee's status and seniority. However, commonly considered benefits are:

- performance bonuses
- overtime payments
- company pension schemes (as well as existing duties to give access to a stake-holder pension)
- contributions to personal pension schemes
- death-in-service life insurance
- private medical cover
- permanent health insurance (PHI) schemes for incapacitated employees
- company cars or car allowances
- share schemes or share/stock option schemes
- season ticket or travelcard loans
- expenses arrangements
- payment of professional course fees (but often with 'claw-back' provision if the employee leaves shortly after the relevant course)
- payment of professional subscriptions
- contractual annual leave entitlements increasing with years of service
- study leave.

### Altering contractual terms

Contractual terms can be varied, but only if the consent of both parties is obtained.

Changes imposed by an employer without the consent of an employee represent a breach of contract and can lead to constructive dismissal claims (i.e. the employee resigning and claiming damages due to the fundamental breach of the contract by the employer). Sometimes, if consent to the suggested change of terms is not forthcoming, it is possible to serve notice upon employees who refuse the new terms that the contract is being brought to an end and to offer them a new contract containing the new terms. However, this must be handled very carefully.

Changes in duties can often constitute changes of a contractual term.

The key to changing terms of employment is to consult effectively with employees before the change is made.

### Consultation

Employees have the right to be consulted during potential dismissal and redundancy situations (see Section 13). In the event of a TUPE transfer (see Section 12), employees have the right to be given key information about the transfer, and often to be consulted on it.

Note that from March 2005 to March 2007, duties will be phased in for employers to inform and consult with staff on business proposals and decisions under the Information and Consultation Regulations 2004. The regulations allow employee representative organisations to be established to take part in consultations. As at 23 March 2005, the Regulations apply to business with 150 or more employees. By 23 March 2007 they will apply to those with 100 or more employees, and by March 2008 to those with 50 or more. See *Where to look* (below) for sources of information about these regulations.

The concept of consultation with staff on important business issues is best practice in any event.

### Wages

Employees have the right to a minimum wage. As at 1 October 2005, this is £5.05 per hour (rising to £5.35 in October 2006); and £3.00 per hour for workers under 18 who are above compulsory school age. Detailed rules apply to what 'pay' counts, but gross pay is used. 'Pay' includes incentive payments, commission and bonuses and also tips and gratuities paid through the payroll. Detailed rules also exist for calculating hours worked for different types of employee. In practice this should not cause difficulties for architects' practices.

Employees have a right to be paid wages for the work they do, and not to have any deductions made from those wages. Deductions can only be made from wages if the employee has given written consent in advance to deductions potentially being made, or if the deduction is made in accordance with a statutory provision (for example the deduction of tax at source).

### Contract termination

Employment contracts can be terminated in the following ways, each of which carries risk:

- dismissal by the employer (with or without notice) (see Section 13, *Dismissals*, page 86)
- resignation by the employee
- expiry and non-renewal of a fixed-term contact
- constructive dismissal (where the employee resigns as a result of a fundamental breach of contract by the employer)
- frustration (where the contract becomes impossible to perform – this is quite rare and is usually due to sickness or imprisonment).

Note the importance, since October 2004, of following a statutory minimum procedure under the statutory disciplinary and dismissal procedures (see Section 13, page 87).

### Architectural students

Architect practices engaging Stage 1/Part I and Stage 2/Part II architectural students enter into short employment contracts. There are a number of issues arising from these contracts.

Essentially, they are fixed-term or specific-purpose contracts in that they last for the duration of training at Stage 1/Part I or Stage 2/Part II level (see Section 6 in relation to fixed-term contracts, page 38).

The RIBA has produced guidance and model contracts for use in relation to Stage 1/Part I and Stage 2/Part II students.

### Checklist

☐ **Provide employees with contracts of employment, setting out tailored clauses, to protect the business and to provide certainty.**

☐ Avoid the uncertainty of verbal contract terms or contractual terms arising through custom and practice.

☐ Include in contracts clauses to satisfy the minimum statutory requirements, but also consider detailed clauses including:

- imposing a probationary period
- restrictions on accepting other work during employment
- requirements to work overtime and undertake other duties
- normal place of work and preserving an ability to move an employee
- confidentiality terms, making clear the types of information which may be treated as confidential to the practice
- obligation for the employee to comply with confidentiality obligations owed by the employer to third parties (for example under the RIBA *Standard Form of Agreement for the Appointment of an Architect* **SFA/99**)
- authority for deductions from wages (e.g. overpayments of holiday pay or expenses)
- payment of RIBA course fees or training fees and claw-back of fees if the employee leaves within a stated period after the fee is paid
- a 'garden leave' clause to force an employee to stay away from work during notice periods
- rules for notification of absence and reporting
- intellectual property terms, clarifying the ownership of employee work and assigning rights to the employer
- data protection terms, giving advanced notice of the purposes for which data may be processed
- restrictive covenants, which need to be carefully drafted, can potentially restrain post-employment competition, solicitation or dealing with and poaching customers and preventing the poaching of key members of staff (see **Section 9,** *Protecting the business*)
- listing potential occurrences that would enable the employer to terminate without notice.

☐ Draft clauses so that they are legally enforceable.

☐ Operate contacts fairly and take implied terms into account, particularly duties of mutual trust and confidence.

☐ The RIBA plans to introduce a model employment contract for use within architects' practices.

☐ Ensure probationary employees are monitored. Do not let a probationary period expire without either confirming full employment, extending the probation or terminating employment.

☐ Decide the link between employment contracts and handbooks and policies (see Section 10). What is to be contractually binding and what is not?

☐ Do not change terms without consultation with employees and without considering the risks of constructive dismissal.

**Where to look**

**Key legislation**

Copyright, Designs and Patents Act 1988
Data Protection Act 1988
Disability Discrimination Acts 1995 and 2005
Employment Act 2002
Employment Act 2002 (Dispute Resolution) Regulations 2004
Employment Equality (Religion or Belief) Regulations 2003
Employment Equality (Sexual Orientation) Regulations 2003
Employment Rights Act 1996
Equal Pay Act 1970
Information and Consultation Regulations 2004
National Minimum Wage Act 1998

**Guidance**

**ACAS**

*Contracts of Employment: getting it right*
*Producing a Written Statement: self-help guide*
*Varying a Contract of Employment*: advice leaflet
ww.acas.org.uk

**Disability Rights Commission**

*Policy Statement on Employment*
www.drc-gb.org

### Department of Trade and Industry

*Contracts of Employment: changes, breaches of contract and deductions from wages*
*Example of a Written Statement*
*Fixed Term Work: a guide to the regulations*
*Guide to Individual Rights of Employees*
*The Law and Best Practice: a detailed guide for employers and part-timers*
*Written Statement of Employment Particulars*
www.dti.gov.uk

### RIBA

*RIBA Employment Policy*
*RIBA Student Employment Contract*
www.riba.org

---

### CASE STUDY

#### Facts

John is a young architect employed by Architect & Partners. He seems trustworthy and is a bright prospect for the future. Architect & Partners does not get round to giving John any form of contract of employment, but does discuss with him a bonus arrangement which will operate after four months of employment. After three months the senior partner of Architect & Partners falls out with John and sacks him without notice. John goes to join a competitor of Architect & Partners.

John successfully sues Architect & Partners for damages for failure to provide him with a Section 1 ERA statement of terms. Further, John argues that the reason he was dismissed was due to racial discrimination on the part of Architect & Partners and recovers substantial damages. He also successfully sues for payment of bonus, which he argues was a contractual term falling due for payment in his notice period.

#### Issues

- A written contract could have provided certainty as to the employment relationship, and could have satisfied Section 1 of the ERA.

CONTINUED ▶

- A probationary period could have provided a valid period in which to monitor performance, and a contractually agreed short notice period during probation.
- The existence of a properly drafted probationary period clause could have assisted in showing the true reason for dismissal, which in itself would assist in defending the race discrimination claim.
- Use of a 'garden leave' clause might have given Architect & Partners a breathing space to cement relationships with clients whilst continuing to keep John employed, subject to contract terms but out of the office – and out of contact with customers.
- Clear remuneration package drafting would have prevented uncertainty as to the bonus arrangement.
- Clear drafting as to notice periods would have prevented argument as to length of notice and benefits falling due in the notice period.

# Section 5

# Discrimination: overview of common concepts

*This section describes issues that are common to all types of discrimination and sets out general matters concerning harassment. Section 6 deals in more detail with some issues relevant to individual types of discrimination (sex, marital status, race, disability, religion, sexual orientation, part-time workers, fixed-term contracts, age and 'whistle-blowing').*

**Issues and alarm bells**

**Discrimination**

Discrimination concerns treating people differently because of certain prohibited reasons: sex, marital status, race, disability, sexual orientation, religion or belief (see Section 6). Plans are in place to expand these prohibitions to include age discrimination (with new age discrimination regulations due to take effect in October 2006). There are also other protections that prevent differences in treatment in a similar way to discrimination laws (for part-time workers, fixed-term contract holders and whistle-blowers (see Section 6).

Discrimination claims can be brought by employees or 'workers' (see Section 2), whether or not currently employed. Former staff members, and even unsuccessful job applicants, can bring discrimination claims.

Employers are responsible for acts of discrimination carried out by employees 'during the course of employment' unless reasonable steps have been taken to prevent discrimination occurring.

If individuals have been discriminated against they can bring damages claims for their losses and for injury to feelings. There is no upper limit on the amount of damages available, and damages for discrimination can be very high.

Different types of discrimination exist: direct, indirect and victimisation. All are equally dangerous, but some are less obvious than others:

- 'Direct' discrimination is taking an action or decision on grounds of a person's characteristics (e.g. because of race or sex).
- 'Indirect' discrimination is (essentially) applying a condition or requirement or following a practice that might seem fine on its face but which actually discriminates because fewer people of a particular kind can comply with it.
- 'Victimisation' is less-favourable treatment because a discrimination claim has been brought or proceedings have been threatened or evidence or information has been given about discrimination.

### Harassment

'Harassment' is a particular form of discrimination which now has a specific definition in European and UK law. The key characteristics of harassment are:

- unwanted conduct which has the 'purpose or effect' of
  - violating dignity, or
  - creating an intimidating, hostile, degrading, humiliating or offensive working environment.

Therefore, harassment can be deliberate or unintentional. Employers are generally liable for the actions of their staff in the workplace, although individual workers should be aware that they can also be personally liable for harassing others. Training is therefore essential to enable staff to recognise and avoid harassment.

### Bullying

'Bullying' is an abuse of power, usually offensive or malicious, intended to injure, undermine or humiliate. There is no freestanding 'bullying' claim available to employees, but it is closely linked to breaches of mutual trust and confidence, discrimination and harassment.

**Checklist**

☐ Establish formal equal opportunities policies to state clearly that discrimination will not be tolerated at any stage of employment.

☐ It is prudent to have separate harassment and bullying policies.

☐ Policies are not enough. Staff need to be aware of the policies and trained to comply with them. The responsibilities of superiors and managers should be clear.

☐ Policies need to be set as standards of behaviour, and linked to disciplinary processes.

☐ Staff should know where and how to complain about discrimination and should be allowed to do so confidentially. The most efficient places to set out information on complaints procedures is in grievance procedures and equal opportunities policies.

☐ Allegations need to be taken seriously and properly investigated.

☐ Staff should be made aware that they can be personally liable for harassment. They should know what can constitute harassment, and particularly that certain actions can constitute harassment even if they are not intended to harass.

☐ Policies should cross-refer to the company grievance and disciplinary procedures, and breaches of policies should be clear disciplinary offences.

☐ Counselling for staff can often assist to diffuse claims.

☐ Monitor existing policies and training to ensure awareness and effectiveness.

☐ Keep records of actions to prove the true reasons for steps taken, so as to combat allegations that acts were on grounds of discrimination. Essentially, you need to be able to prove that an employee would have been treated in the same way irrespective of their sex, race, disability, etc.

**Where to look**

Refer to Section 6 for key legislation and guidance.

# Section 6
# Discrimination: specifics

*This section deals with specific issues relevant to specific types of discrimination, and best practice to avoid discrimination allegations. See Section 5 for general issues and alarm bells common to any type of discrimination.*

**Issues and alarm bells**

**Sex or marital status**

Sex discrimination arises in relation to:

- a person's gender (treating males and females differently)
- marital status (treating a married person differently to a single person)
- pregnancy-related discrimination (which clearly discriminates against females only)
- dealing with flexible working requests (e.g. to work part-time on return from maternity leave) (see also Section 7)
- direct or indirect harassment or victimisation on grounds of sex or marital status (see Section 5).

Transsexuals are now protected. Discrimination against someone who intends to undergo, is undergoing or has undergone gender reassignment is outlawed because it is essentially discrimination on the grounds of sex.

Indirect sex discrimination applies to the application of a 'provision, criteria or practice' that (essentially) is to the detriment of a considerably larger proportion of women than men (or vice versa) or married people than single people.

Employers can defend sex discrimination if there is a 'genuine occupational qualification' for the job. Examples would include a requirement for male workers for male hospitals or prisons, where single-sex accommodation is provided in a job where living on site is essential, or where physical strength is needed or physical contact is required.

**Race discrimination**

Race discrimination arises in relation to differential treatment on 'racial grounds' (colour, race, nationality, ethnic or national origins) or for being part of a 'racial group'. Racial groups include Sikhs, Jews, Romany gypsies and Scots (as distinct from English). Rastafarians are not an ethnic group. 'Colour' can comprise more than one racial group or origin.

Direct and indirect harassment and victimisation on grounds of race are prohibited (see Section 5).

Indirect race discrimination (other than on grounds of colour or nationality) applies (essentially) to the application of a 'provision, criteria or practice' that puts people of different races or ethnic or national origins at a disadvantage compared with others and which the employer cannot justify as a proportionate means of achieving a legitimate aim.

Indirect race discrimination for colour and nationality applies if a detrimental 'requirement or condition' is applied and with which a considerably smaller proportion of people of a particular colour or nationality can comply and which the employer cannot justify.

Employers can defend race discrimination if a 'genuine occupational qualification' exists. Being a particular race in a job can be a valid requirement if it is proportionate. In situations other than discrimination for race or ethnic or national origins, further rules apply based on specific needs of the business (for example, dramatic performances or the need for employees of a particular nationality to work in restaurants). Few, if any, will apply to architects' practices.

**Disability discrimination**

The Disability Discrimination Act 1995 governs discrimination against 'disabled' people in the provisions of services generally (with which architects will be familiar) and discrimination in the workplace. This section deals with the parts of that Act relevant to employment, as opposed to the parts dealing with the specific duties service providers owe to the public.

The Act now applies to employers of all sizes; the small employer exemption has been removed.

The definition of 'disability' is far wider than might be expected, but it does not cover all medical conditions. The essential parts are (in summary):

- a physical or mental impairment which
  - lasts or is likely to last 12 months or will recur, and
  - affects normal day-to-day activities.

Normal day-to-day activities are normal actions, not necessary work activities. They include:

- movement
- normal manual dexterity
- physical coordination
- continence
- ability to lift or move everyday objects
- speech, hearing and eyesight
- memory and ability to learn, concentrate or understand
- perception of risk or physical danger.

The effect of treatment is discounted except in the case of correction for poor eyesight.

Beware of signs of disability or where you are on notice of disability or illness. Each case is different, and all of the following have been found to be 'disabilities':

- dyslexia
- HIV
- cancer
- migraine suffering
- back pain
- epilepsy
- claustrophobia.

Direct and indirect victimisation and harassment on grounds of disability all apply.

Employers are also under duties to make 'reasonable adjustments' for disabled employees. Failure to do this is a form of discrimination in itself. Whether an adjustment is reasonable will depend on cost, practicalities and the size of the business, but examples of potential adjustments are:

- physical building adjustments (e.g. ramps, light switches, door widening, rails, lifts)
- different work hours, shifts or patterns
- extra training (e.g. in using extra equipment)
- extra equipment (e.g. IT packages to assist dyslexic employees)
- modified tools or equipment (e.g. chairs for back pain)
- rooms without bright lights, for interviewing an epileptic.

Note the close link between disability discrimination and long-term sickness and absence monitoring (see Section 8, page 56). They key is to consider potential disabilities and potential adjustments as separate but related issues.

### Religion

This is a new area of discrimination legislation, which may well lead to increased claims against companies. It should be considered seriously.

The prohibition is against discrimination on grounds of religion or religious belief or other similar philosophical belief. This includes correct or incorrect perceptions, or acts based on a person's association with another person of a particular religion or belief.

The definition is wide-ranging and untested. It could include organised religions, non-conventional factors or alternative lifestyles, non-believers, atheism, paganism and humanism. However, it does not include political beliefs.

Direct discrimination, indirect discrimination (unless justifiable as a proportionate means of achieving a legitimate aim), victimisation and harassment are all outlawed, although limited 'genuine occupational requirements' apply.

ACAS guidance explains the problems well and sets out examples of the beliefs of different religions (see *Where to look*, below). It is essential that these are understood by managers.

Potential problem areas include:

- dress codes
- holidays, time off, breaks (especially religious holidays and prayer times)

- closure periods
- recruitment
- religious leave requests
- social interaction (e.g. company events)
- certain foods being alien to different religions (and therefore related problems in storing food and serving food at work functions)
- alcohol issues (e.g. appropriate venues for events and meetings)
- prayer rooms/quiet areas.

Specific exemptions exist to allow Sikhs on construction sites not to wear safety helmets.

**Sexual orientation**

This is another new area of discrimination legislation, with similar structure and issues to religious discrimination.

'Sexual orientation' relates to an individual's preference for persons:

- of the same sex (lesbian and gay)
- of the opposite sex (heterosexual)
- of the same and the opposite sex (bisexual).

Different treatment on grounds of sexual orientation is prohibited unless justified as a proportionate means of achieving a legitimate business aim. Prohibited grounds would also include, for example, a heterosexual man's friendship with a gay man, or an incorrect perception that a man is gay.

Direct and indirect discrimination, victimisation and harassment concepts all apply.

Potential problem areas include:

- the link between sexual orientation and religious beliefs about sexual orientation
- recruitment, advertising, interviewing and selection (see Section 3)
- benefits to same-sex partners
- dealing with suspicions of sexual orientation
- gathering information (e.g. do you really need to know about marital status, or to have contact details of those with whom a person lives?).

Very limited and controversial 'genuine occupational requirements' exist (which will not apply to architects' practices). There is also a defence if the employer took reasonable steps to prevent an employee from acting in a discriminatory manner.

An exemption exists for benefits dependent on marital status (for example, occupational pension schemes which are only available to widowers).

ACAS has issued guidelines on discrimination based on sexual orientation (see *Where to look*, below).

**Part-time workers**

Part-time workers are now specifically protected by law in relation to pay and detrimental treatment. In basic terms, a part-time worker (i.e. one treated as less than full-time by a business) cannot be detrimentally treated compared with a full-time worker.

Part-time workers can compare themselves to full-time workers who are:

- employed under the 'same type of contract' (apprentices are deemed not to be the same as non-apprentices, 'workers' are deemed not to be the same as employees)
- employed in the same or broadly similar work (including relevant qualifications, skills and experience levels)
- based at the same 'establishment'.

To win a claim, a part-time worker must also show that the treatment was on the grounds that he or she is part-time, and that the treatment could not be justified by the company on objective business grounds.

It is acceptable to set levels of pay and benefits on a pro rata basis, in line with working hours, if appropriate.

**Fixed-term contracts**

People working on fixed-term contracts have had protection against discrimination since October 2002 by statutory regulations. Some apprentices, work experience students and trainees are excluded. Seasonal or casual staff are usually included.

For the purposes of the regulations, 'fixed-term' contracts include:

- contracts for a defined period (whether or not notice can be given earlier)
- contracts for a specific act or task
- contracts ending on the happening of an event.

A fixed-term worker cannot be treated less favourably than a comparative permanent employee engaged in the same or similar work and in the same work establishment. Not renewing a fixed-term contract is not detrimental treatment in itself. Note, however, that dismissing an employee because a fixed-term contract is not being renewed is now one of the types of dismissals that must be dealt with under the new statutory dismissal and disciplinary procedures (which involve advanced warning, a meeting to discuss and a right of appeal – see Section 13, page 88).

Benefits can be genuinely applied on a pro rata basis.

A notable difference to other forms of discrimination is that justification of different treatment to proportionately achieve a necessary business objective includes an ability to say there has been an offset; in other words, even though detrimental treatment has taken place, the fixed-term worker is as well off overall as a comparative employee. An example would be not giving a fixed-term worker a company car, but giving him or her an added cash benefit instead.

The historic practice of workers agreeing to exclude unfair dismissal or redundancy claims if fixed-term contracts expire without renewal is now illegal (unless in the case of redundancy the contract was agreed or extended before 1 October 2002).

Successive reviewed fixed-term contracts can only last for four years. After four years, the contract becomes indefinite and subject to notice.

**Age discrimination**

The UK Government has been consulting on the introduction of regulations governing age discrimination with a view to implementing new regulations in October 2006. As at the time of completing this text, new draft regulations have been published.

Discrimination on grounds of age (young or old) will be outlawed, except where employers can justify it on specific grounds. A statutory retirement age (probably 65) will be set, and employers will need to justify an earlier retirement age. Employees will be able to apply to retire later. Unfair dismissal and redundancy rights (see Section 13) will be available to employees over 65 (unlike now). The latest draft regulations introduce the new concept of a 'planned retirement', which will constitute a fair dismissal as long as it takes place on or after the statutory retirement age (or an employer's other justified age) as long as a specified procedure is followed, including giving the employee between 6 and 12 months notice of the planned retirement.

Certain jobs will clearly require adequate experience, but care will be needed to ensure that this does not turn into a minimum age requirement.

**Whistle-blowers**

Since the Public Interest Disclosure Act 1998, workers who properly raise issues about wrongdoing in a company are protected from detrimental treatment. The rights are highly complex, but the alarm bell to businesses is to take 'whistle-blowers' seriously and check that the correct procedures are followed.

Workers' protection only applies to 'protected disclosures' (which include alleged criminal offences, breaches of legal obligations, health and safety problems and cover-ups). Workers cannot 'blow the whistle' to just anybody. There is a pecking order, starting first with disclosure to the employer internally. Disclosures straight to the media are well down the list. It is slightly easier to disclose to a list of pre-scribed persons, such as the Health and Safety Executive, Food Standards Agency and HM Revenue and Customs, but the worker needs to pass various tests to retain protection.

If workers know that there is a proper whistle-blowers' policy, which encourages them to raise issues in a regulated manner, issues can often dealt with internally in an efficient manner.

**Checklist**

**General**

☐ **Review practices in line with the Checklist in Section 5.**

☐ **Monitor the application of any 'provision, criteria or practice' to ensure there is no indirect discrimination.**

☐ **Remember the potential discriminatory nature of advertisements and job interview processes (see Section 3).**

☐ **Take care in implementing dress codes. They may discriminate on sex, race and religious grounds. Dress codes can often be enforced for food hygiene reasons, as uniforms to signify a company or a status, or simply to ensure** appropriate standards of dress. The key is to be able to justify the dress requirement on business grounds, so that comparative people (for example, men and women) are treated in an equivalent manner to enforce a common business aim or standard.

☐ Remember that many potential discrimination and harassment issues can be dealt with effectively at the outset by openly consulting affected staff, assessing the wishes of the individual, carrying out adequate investigations and being seen to take issues seriously.

## Disability

☐ Management should understand the definition of 'disability' and take care to consider the risks of actions in relation to those with disabilities.

☐ Keep records to prove consideration of 'reasonable adjustments' for disabled employees, even if you decide it is not reasonable to make any such adjustments.

## Religion

☐ Management should be educated about potential traps for religious discrimination. In particular, review the ACAS guidance, which sets out the main differences in practices and beliefs of different religions.

☐ Review policies and practices to ensure they do not offend different religions or beliefs.

## Sexual orientation

☐ Review policies and practices to ensure they do not offend people of different sexual orientations.

☐ Consider policies concerning information gathering (for example, staff contact numbers, etc.) to ensure the information is really important and is, in any event, kept confidential on a 'need to know' basis.

## Part-time workers

☐ Ensure that part-time workers are not treated differently on the sole ground that they are part-time, unless it is justifiable.

### Fixed-**term contracts**

☐ Review benefits and arrangements for workers with fixed-term contracts to ensure discrimination does not arise.

☐ Review renewals of fixed-term contracts to monitor whether four-years' worth of renewals have created a permanent contract.

☐ Factor in minimum statutory dismissal hearings at the end of a fixed-term contract.

### Age discrimination

☐ Think now about the effect of age discrimination legislation, which is expected to be in force from October 2006. As regulations are drafted, adapt working practices and any benefits that are dependent on age, as well as recruitment, promotion and reward practices.

### Whistle-blowers

☐ Ensure that proper procedures are in place to enable whistle-blowers to raise issues and retain confidentiality and protection. Do not simply ignore a whistle-blower; investigate, and check that the correct procedures are followed.

### Where to look

### Key legislation

Age Discrimination (No. 2) Bill
Disability Discrimination Acts 1995 and 2005
Employment Equality (Religion or Belief) Regulations 2003
Employment Equality (Sexual Orientation) Regulations 2003
Protection from Harassment Act 1997
Public Interest Disclosure Act 1998
Public Interest Disclosure (Prescribed Persons) Order 1999 (as amended)
Race Relations Act 1976 (as amended)
Sex Discrimination Act 1975 (as amended)

### Guidance

ACAS
*The A–Z of Work*: advisory handbook

*Bullying and Harassment at Work: guide for managers and employers*
*Changing Patterns of Work*: booklet
*Religion or Belief and the Workplace*
*Sexual Orientation and the Workplace*
*Tackling Discrimination and Promoting Equality*: advisory booklet
www.acas.org.uk

### Department of Trade and Industry (DTI)

*Age Diversity in Employment – code of practice*
*Coming of Age: consultation on the draft Employment Equality (Age) Regulations 2006*
*Equality and Diversity: age discrimination in employment and vocational training*
www.dti.org.uk

### Public Concern at Work

www.pcaw.co.uk

### RIBA

*Why Women Leave Architecture*
www.riba.org

### Trades Union Congress (TUC)

TUC Briefing on Government Age Equality Consultation
www.tuc.org.uk

See also Section 2 *Employee status* and Section 7 *Family-friendly and flexible work issues*.

---

**CASE STUDY**

**Facts**

Architect & Partners undertook a review of working practices and noticed that many more clients are working at weekends. As a result, the firm implemented a new provision whereby employees are asked to work at weekends when the need arises. Although the provision does not amount to a requirement of the firm, in practice the situation arises whereby employees are frowned upon, and deemed to be unwilling performers, if they refuse to carry out weekend work.

CONTINUED ▶

---

**CASE STUDY (CONTINUED)**

### Issues

- Although the weekend working is not a requirement, it could constitute a 'provision, criteria or practice'.
- The firm runs a high risk of female workers arguing that they are less likely to be able to comply than men due to childcare duties, and that the practice that has arisen means they are being detrimentally treated in being frowned upon for failing to work on weekend projects.
- Firms should always second guess the effects of their working practices to ensure they are not indirectly discriminatory on any grounds.

# Section 7
# Family-friendly and flexible work issues

*This section brings together a variety of rights and considerations that can fall into the category of 'family friendly'. In recent times the traditional idea of a 'family' has been extended, as has the wish for employees to change their work–life balance. Employers should also understand the benefits to be gained by allowing employees to work flexibly in the right circumstances, and the fact that work life and family life are complementary; parenthood, for example, can often bring with it a more motivated employee.*

**Issues and alarm bells**

**Maternity rights**

The statutory rights given to employees who are pregnant, on maternity leave or returning from maternity leave are complex and constantly changing. Advice should always be taken. However, much good guidance exists (see *Where to look*, below).

All employees are entitled to 26 weeks of 'ordinary maternity leave'. Some employees are also entitled to a further period of 26 weeks of 'additional maternity leave', depending on their length of service (currently, 26 weeks' continuous service is needed at a point 14 weeks before the expected week of childbirth). Note that the Government is currently proposing to extend these entitlements further.

Specific protection provisions for employees relating to maternity include the following:

- The right not to be treated detrimentally or dismissed due to pregnancy or maternity.
- Automatic unfair dismissal rights (see Section 13, page 86) irrespective of length of service if the reason for dismissal is pregnancy or maternity.

- The right to return to the same job after ordinary maternity leave.
- Employment terms and conditions and benefits continue to apply in the ordinary maternity leave period, except for pay.

Factors that affect the level of protection during maternity include the following:

- Pay during the ordinary and additional maternity periods can be agreed between employer and employee in a contract. However, the employee must at least be paid statutory maternity pay during ordinary maternity leave (see *Where to look*, below, for where to find current levels of pay).
- Only some terms and conditions of employment operate during additional maternity leave.
- There is significant overlap between maternity rights and rights not to be discriminated against on grounds of sex or marital status (see Section 6, page 33). Both rights need to be considered.
- New employees can be recruited to cover for employees on maternity leave. However, their terms of engagement and the purpose and duration of employment need to be very clear.
- Dismissal of a pregnant employee or an employee who is on maternity leave can be fair as long as the dismissal is not by reason of or related to pregnancy or maternity. A true redundancy position is an example, but consultation must be adopted to take account of the employee's condition or the fact that she is not physically attending the office, and employees on maternity leave have the right to be offered suitable alternative jobs that may exist.

**Adoption leave**

Both male and female employees have rights to take adoption leave, which are similar to maternity leave rights. Similar periods of 26 weeks' ordinary adoption leave and 26 weeks' unpaid adoption leave exist for current levels of statutory adoption leave pay (see *Where to look*, below).

To be eligible for adoption leave employees must have:

- 26 weeks' continuous service with the employer at the end of the week in which the employee is matched for adoption, and
- been matched for adoption by an adoption agency.

If a couple have been matched for adoption, only one member of the couple can elect to take adoption leave.

**Paternity leave**

Paternity leave rights are available to certain employees to care for a newborn or adopted child or its mother. Paternity leave is available not only to the father of a child, but also to the husband or partner of a child's mother, as long as he has 26 weeks' continuous employment with his employer and will have responsibilities for bringing up the child.

A 'partner' for these purposes is a person living with and in an enduring family relationship with the mother, but who is not a relative of the mother.

The leave is paid for two weeks at a relatively low statutory paternity pay level (see *Where to look*, below, for where to find the latest levels of pay), although many employers agree to pay more than this or to pay for a longer period of time.

Staff are protected from being detrimentally treated for requesting or taking paternity leave. Note that 'paternity leave' is different to 'parental leave' (see below).

**Parental leave**

Parental leave is a right to take unpaid leave to care for a young child. There are only certain periods in which parental leave can be taken, which are:

- up to 5 years from the date of birth, or
- up to 5 years from the date of placement for adoption (or up to the adopted child's eighteenth birthday).

Employees are protected from detrimental treatment arising from requesting or taking parental leave, and in essence are entitled to a guaranteed right to return to the same or similar job after parental leave.

The relevant statutory regulations provide that parental leave can only be taken for certain periods, unless otherwise agreed between employer and employee – see *Where to look*, below, for details of the provisions in the Maternity and Parental Leave (Amendment) Regulations 2002. In short:

- leave can only be taken in blocks or multiples of one week
- a maximum of four weeks may be taken in any one year
- 21-days' notice must be given
- there is some leeway for employers to postpone leave for business reasons.

## Dependants leave

Employees have the right to a reasonable amount of time off work to take necessary actions to care for 'dependants'. Time off can only be taken to deal with certain events (see below). In essence, these are emergency events.

A 'dependant' is the wife, husband, child or parent of an employee, or someone living in the same household (but not an employee, tenant, lodger or boarder) or someone who reasonably relies on the employee for assistance when the person falls ill or is injured, or to provide care in the event of injury or illness.

See *Where to look*, below, for sources of information setting out the full list of events in respect of which dependants leave can be taken. In essence they are;

- to provide assistance in the event of illness, injury or assault, or if a dependant gives birth
- to make arrangements for care to be provided to an ill or injured dependant
- following the death of a dependant
- due to unexpected disruption or termination of care arrangements
- to deal with an incident involving a child occurring unexpectedly in a period when the child's school or educational establishment is responsible for the child.

Employees must tell employers about the time off as soon as reasonably practical (note that in some circumstances this might be after the leave has been commenced or taken).

## Flexible working requests

Certain employees are entitled to request to work 'flexibly' (i.e. to seek a variation to their hours or patterns of work, or to seek time off work or to work at home). This can include job shares and flexible working hours. Such requests must be taken seriously. There is a specified format for dealing with requests.

Flexible working requests can overlap significantly with sex discrimination rights (see Sections 5 and 6), especially in the case of female employees requesting to work flexibly after returning from maternity leave.

Only the following people can request to work flexibly:

- employees
  - with 26 weeks' continuous service

- who are a parent, adopter, foster parent or guardian (or a partner of such a person)
- who has a child under 6 years of age (or under 18 if the child is disabled).

Under the Flexible Working (Eligibility, Complaints and Remedies) Regulations 2002, full procedures are required to operate in relation to flexible work requests (see *Where to look*, below). In essence:

- the employee must set out in writing why the request is being made and the effect it might have on the employer's business
- meetings must be held with the employee to discuss the request
- the employee must have the right to be accompanied at the meetings by a fellow work colleague or a trade union official
- an appeal against any refusal must be allowed.

Employers can only refuse flexible working requests on specific business grounds, summarised as follows:

- the burden of additional costs to the employer
- a detrimental effect on the employer's ability to meet customer demand
- the employer's inability to reorganise work amongst existing staff
- the employer's inability to recruit additional staff to accommodate the flexible working request
- detrimental impact on the quality of service provided by the employer
- detrimental impact on the performance of the employer's business as a result of the flexible working arrangement
- insufficient work for the employee to do in the periods the employee proposes to work
- planned structural changes within the employer's business.

**Homeworking**

Employers may agree that workers can work at home for some or all of their working week. However, homeworking brings with it various issues and duties for the employer to consider.

Key issues to address in relation to homeworking are:

- employees should use the employer's work property (computers, etc.) at home
- the working environment should be risk assessed

- particular areas of importance are computer system suitability, display screen suitability, adjustable chairs, systems for reporting accidents, assessing ventilation and heat, and implementing rest breaks.

It should also be noted that:

- risk assessments of homeworking environments are statutory health and safety requirements
- tax implications can arise from using part of a home for homeworking
- employment contracts need to be changed to reflect homeworking duties and place of work
- the employer should retain a contractual right to enter an employee's home to recover the employer's property
- home insurance policies are unlikely to be comprehensive enough to cover working at home; suitable policies should be taken out to cover the risks of homeworking and home offices.

## Checklist

☐ Become familiar with 'family-friendly' rights. It is better to plan in advance how to deal with them, rather than to react once a situation or request arises.

☐ Ensure that employees on maternity leave are:

- included in pay reviews
- paid bonuses
- informed of vacancies or chances of promotion notified to other employees
- consulted with fairly if restructuring or redundancies are envisaged, and permitted to take suitable alternative jobs which may be available.

☐ Take care when appointing replacement employees to cover for maternity leave. Their terms of engagement should be made very clear.

☐ Proper maternity policies can assist in making an employer's processes and procedures clear and understandable to staff.

☐ Policies should be adapted to set out adoption leave rights.

☐ Do not assume that fathers do not have paternity leave rights. Understand the rights and consider granting clear contractual paternity leave and paternity pay rights.

☐ It is best to adopt a clear policy for parental leave, dealing in particular with otherwise unclear areas such as how to request leave, the required notice to be given approval of leave, and how much leave can be taken at one time.

☐ Take care in dealing with requests for time off to deal with emergencies involving dependants. Do not assume that employees are not entitled to such leave.

☐ Do not ignore or instantly reject requests to work flexibly. Many managers instantly say 'no'. This is highly dangerous. Understand and implement the terms of the Flexible Working (Eligibility, Complaints and Remedies) Regulations 2002, especially if requests to work part-time or flexibly are received from employees returning from maternity leave. Train managers in this area to increase awareness.

☐ Assess the homeworking conditions of homeworkers and implement suitable changes to homeworking environments, employment contracts and insurance arrangements.

☐ Take care not to take any steps that might treat part-time workers detrimentally. There can be a tendency to treat part-time workers as less important than full-time workers, and in effect to 'demote' a person who switches to part-time status.

☐ Take care in assessing flexible working requests, even if at first the request might appear unreasonable. For example, do not assume that a project architect's request for flexible working arrangements should be refused. As with all other flexible working requests, there are a number of factors that could be considered to assist with flexible working, such as enhancing mobile phone and mobile e-mail capabilities and viewing timekeeping issues realistically.

**Where to look**

**Legislation**

Employment Act 2002
Employment Act 2002 (Dispute Resolution) Regulations 2004
Employment Relations Act 2004
Employment Rights Act 1996

Flexible Working (Eligibility, Complaints and Remedies) Regulations 2002
Human Rights Act 1998
Maternity and Parental Leave etc. Regulations 1999 (as amended)
Paternity and Adoption Leave Regulations 2002

## Guidance

### ACAS

*Changing Patterns of Work: advice booklet*
*Flexible Working:* advice leaflet
www.acas.org.uk

### Department of Trade and Industry

*Adoptive Parents: rights to leave and pay when a child is placed for adoption within the UK*
*Flexible Working: best practice forms*
*Flexible Working: the right to request and the duty to consider: guidance for employers and employees*
*Flexible Working – The Right to Request: a basic summary*
*Maternity Rights: a guide for employers and employees*
*Model Letter for Employers to Acknowledge Notification of Maternity Leave*
*Parental Leave: detailed guidance for employers and employees*
*Time Off for Dependants: a guide for employers and employees*
*Working Fathers: rights to paternity leave and pay*
www.dti.gov.uk/er/

### Tailored Interactive Guidance on Employment Rights (TIGER)

www.tiger.gov.uk
Equal Opportunities Commission
Advice on family-friendly policies
www.eoc.org.uk

### Health and Safety Executive

*A Guide for New and Expectant Mothers Who Work*
www.hse.gov.uk

# Section 8
# Health, safety and welfare in the workplace

*This section deals with a number of different areas that are related to the issue of workplace health and safety. In addition to pure health and safety duties, this section covers working time legislation, sickness and absence, and stress at work. Understanding and monitoring these issues assists employers significantly in developing an effective workforce, with resulting positive benefits for a business.*

## Issues and alarm bells

### Working time

The Working Time Regulations 1998 impact on all business. They regulate hours of work, rest breaks and holidays and are closely allied to health and safety duties. The relevant time is 'working time' – not all hours count as 'working time'. 'Working time' is time working at the employer's disposal and carrying out activities or duties; therefore, it will usually not include travel to or from work, time during rest breaks, or time on call off-site if the worker is free to pursue leisure activities.

Although the regulations do not yet fully apply to all business sectors, they apply in full to architecture and related professions. The regulations protect employees and 'workers' (see Section 2, page 6) but not the genuinely self-employed.

Parts of the regulations are detailed and complex. The basics rights are:

- not to work more than 48 hours a week on average in total – even if a worker works for more than one employer
- an ability to opt out of the 48-hour week (the European Union is pressing to ban this)
- 11 hours of rest between working days
- 20-minute rest break in any six-hour working period (which is usually covered by a lunch break)

- adequate rest during monotonous work
- a statutory right to four weeks' annual leave (not including bank holidays).

Some hours of work are 'unmeasured', either because the worker is exempt because his or her work is not measured or predetermined, or because the worker can regulate his or her own hours (an 'autonomous decision taker', for example, a managing director). Also, some hours themselves are exempt because the worker voluntarily chooses to work outside the hours predetermined by the employer. The 'extra' hours then do not count as working hours at all.

In some 'special' situations, workers can be asked to continue working without breaks, but at the end an equivalent rest break ('compensatory rest') must be given as soon as practicable. Such special cases include:

- unusual and unforeseeable circumstances
- foreseeable surges of activity
- where service continuity is needed (e.g. prisons, hospitals and factories needing to run machines)
- if permanent presence is needed (e.g. security, maintenance).

The statutory annual leave is four weeks (being four weeks in terms of the worker's normal week; for example, a two-day week part-time worker is entitled to eight days' holiday). Statutory holidays are a minimum level of holiday entitlement; contractual holiday benefits can, and often do, exceed statutory holidays, in which case the statutory entitlement becomes irrelevant.

Records must be kept to show whether the 48-hour limits are being complied with.

Specific rules exist relating to night workers (those who work in a period of not less than seven hours including the period between midnight and 5 a.m.). Special rules also apply to young persons (i.e. a person above compulsory school age but under 18).

**Health and safety**

A detailed review of the numerous health and safety obligations imposed on employers is beyond the scope of this guide. However, main issues of concern to an employer in relation to employees include the following:

- Employers must:

- ensure the health, safety and welfare of employees
- ensure safe systems of work, safe handling and storage, adequate information and training, safe places of work and a safe working environment
- undertake appropriate risk assessments, including health surveillance and specific assessments for new or expectant mothers
- have procedures to deal with serious and imminent danger
- provide employees with adequate details of risks (based on risk assessments and in a comprehensible form) and train them adequately
- protect the health and safety of architects' staff when engaged on site visits
- provide necessary protective equipment
- provide training to staff and management in relation to health and safety duties.

- Employees must:

  - not endanger themselves by their acts or omissions
  - co-operate with their employer on health and safety matters (e.g. by wearing hard hats or other personal protection).

- Many health and safety duties are based on the need to take such steps as are 'reasonably practicable'. Disproportionate cost and inconvenience is relevant, but the balance is to be made against the risk to health and safety.

**Sickness and absence**

Employees are entitled to statutory sick pay (SSP) when sick (see *Where to look*, below, for sources of current levels of SSP). Commonly, contractual sick pay exceeds SSP benefits in any event.

Sickness absences must be investigated and handled carefully. There is a significant crossover to the following:

- disability discrimination (Section 6)
- discipline and dismissal (Section 13)
- stress (see below).

The key to managing absences is communication; discussing the reasons for absence with the employee, even on his or her return after one day off.

Different types of absences require different considerations. Be prepared to categorise absences and review appropriate actions as follows:

- Long-term absence – the person may be 'disabled' (see Section 6), or in any event could become incapable of working. Medical evidence is essential to establish cause and prognosis. Special rules exist for obtaining medical reports (Access to Medical Records Act 1988).
- Short-term absence – if authorised (in that absence reporting procedures have been followed), the key is to establish whether there is an underlying medical reason.
- Short-term unconnected absences – if unauthorised, disciplinary or dismissal action may be appropriate (see Section 13); if authorised, but the illnesses are unconnected, patterns of illness can be reviewed, and if it is deemed that the absences are unrelated the situation may constitute a misconduct issue (not a sickness issue at all), meriting disciplinary warnings or dismissal.

ACAS guidance exists for handling the above scenarios (see *Where to look*, below).

For all such absences, return-to-work meetings with management are essential to enable proper investigation, support and decisions to be taken.

Truly sick employees can be dismissed if a proper process is followed, but only if the employer has obtained and considered medical evidence, considered how long the business can reasonably be expected to wait, considered alternative positions for the employee and (particularly if a 'disability' exists) considered whether reasonable adjustments can be made. Dismissal may be possible if the business cannot reasonably wait for the employee's return.

Difficulties can arise in dismissing sick employees who otherwise would reach a period of successive illness so as to benefit from a permanent health insurance (PHI) scheme operated by the employer.

**Stress at work**

Stress in the workplace has been highly publicised due to some large damages awards paid to employees who are 'stressed'.

Employers must be conscious of the issues relating to stress at work. However, employees can only succeed in claims if they have been foreseeably injured (physically or mentally) because of stress which is due to employer negligence or breach of duty towards employees.

It is vital to remember that stress is not an illness. It is an adverse reaction to pressures or demands, and can be caused by home/external pressures as well as work. Management should be trained to spot typical stress-induced illnesses (for example, anxiety, headaches, irritability, depression, boredom, fatigue, heavy smoking, heavy drinking, sleeping problems and long-term heart disease, hypertension, gastric and internal problems, insomnia, clinical depression, neurosis). Managers should watch out for unaccustomed gloominess, irritability, tiredness, lapses in concentration, poor time-keeping, erratic decision-making, recourse to or dependency on alcohol and lack of enthusiasm.

Train management also to spot 'stressors', which may or may not be related to work. Typical stressors include:

- culture and long hours
- job demands
- workload too heavy or too light
- control – lack of flexibility, heavy supervision
- relationships – bullying, lack of recognition
- change – job insecurity
- role issues – unclear job descriptions, lack of career prospects, lack of support.

The court judgments for key cases list the relevant considerations for deciding whether an employee can succeed in a stress-related injury claim (see *Where to look*, below, and in particular the cases of *Sutherland* v. *Hatton* [2002] EWCA GU 76 CA 05/02/02 and *Barber* v. *Somerset County Council* [2004] UKHL13). In particular:

- the employer must have been negligent
- injury must be foreseeable by the employer
- no job is inherently stressful, and employees are expected to withstand reasonable pressure unless the employer knows about particular vulnerabilities
- greater issues arise if any demands are unreasonable or if an employee is known to have suffered stress-induced illness before
- employers can only be expected to take reasonable steps which do some good
- providing confidential advice services or helplines can greatly help employers against breach of duty allegations.

Stress issues cross over with other duties, such as the duty of good faith (Section 4), working hours (Section 8), ill health (dismissals and sickness, Sections 8 and 13), disability (Section 6), conduct and discipline (Sections 8 and 13) and bullying and harassment (Section 5).

The Health and Safety Executive (HSE) has introduced new management standards for assessing the work environment and managing stress. Compliance with this can greatly assist employers in defending claims.

## Checklist

### Working time

- [ ] Monitor practices to establish compliance with the Working Time Regulations 1998.

- [ ] Establish time-recording processes to enable monitoring of working hours. Staff should record all hours, not just the hours they are contracted to work.

- [ ] Review or implement 48-hour week opt-out agreements (until such time as the planned ban on the 48-hour week opt-out is implemented).

- [ ] Review contractual holiday rights to ensure they cover statutory holiday rights as a minimum. Consider contractual holiday rights that increase as service increases.

- [ ] Government regulations on record keeping are changing. The best advice is to record all hours, even if 48-hour week opt-outs are in place.

### Health and safety

- [ ] Establish, implement and review proper health and safety statements and practices. Bring policies to the attention of staff and train staff in their implementation.

- [ ] Understand the need to carry out risk assessments, and take action to implement effective assessments.

### Sickness and absence

- [ ] Monitor absences effectively and deal with sickness absences carefully in the appropriate manner to fit the type of absence. Establish processes for communication with absent staff, and hold return-to-work meetings.

- [ ] Establish processes to support the well-being of absent staff, ensuring they are balanced against monitoring the reason for absence. Keep effective records to validate later actions.

**Stress**

☐ **Take management steps to understand symptoms of stress and 'stressors' (factors that typically lead to workplace stress).**

☐ **Provide access to confidential counselling phone lines or services for stressed employees to contact.**

☐ **Introduce stress management into health and safety policies.**

☐ **Comply with the new HSE management standards.**

**Where to look**

**Key legislation**

Access to Medical Records Act 1988
Construction (Design and Management) Regulations 1994
Disability Discrimination Acts 1995 and 2005
Health and Safety at Work etc. Act 1974
Employers' Liability (Compulsory Insurance) Act 1969
Employers' Liability (Compulsory Insurance) Regulations 1988
Management of Health and Safety at Work Regulations 1999
Noise at Work Regulations 1989
Occupiers' Liability Acts 1957 and 1984
Social Security Contributions and Benefits Act 1992 (as amended)
Work at Height Regulations
Working Time Regulations 1998
Workplace (Health, Safety and Welfare) Regulations 1992

**Guidance**

**ACAS**

*Bullying and Harassment at Work: a guide for managers and employees*
*Health and Employment: advisory booklet*
*Holidays and Holiday Pay: advisory leaflet*
*Personnel Data and Record Keeping: advisory booklet*
www.acas.org.uk

***Barber** v. Somerset County Council*
House of Lords judgment
www.parliament.the-stationery-office.co.uk

### Department of Health
*Choosing Health: making healthier choices easier*
www.dh.gov.uk

### Department for Work and Pensions
Advice on statutory sick pay, including current rates, from the DWP website
www.dwp.gov.uk

### Department of Trade and Industry
*Your Guide to the Working Time Regulations*
www.dti.gov.uk

### Health and Safety Executive
Management Standards for Work-Related Stress
www.hse.gov.uk

### *Sutherland v. Hatton*
House of Lords judgment
www.lawreports.co.uk

# Section 9
# Protecting the business

*This section reviews methods of protection of employers' interests in property such as confidential information, client and customer connections, and intellectual property, as well as issues surrounding monitoring staff in order to protect legitimate interests.*

**Issues and alarm bells**

**'Property'**

Companies are entitled to protect company property. Property comes in various forms; typical 'property' valued by architects' practices includes:

- client relationships
- confidential information (including drawings)
- copyright and other intellectual property
- physical property (computers, company cars, etc.)
- established company workforces.

All these forms of property can be protected to a certain extent. Set out below is a basic summary of methods of protection. Ensuring protections are enforceable and taking steps to enforce them is a specialist area, and practices are encouraged to take legal advice on such issues.

**Restraint of trade and restrictive covenants**

Employees are subject to an implied duty not to compete with the business of their employers during employment.

Clauses can be drafted into employment contracts to prevent employees who leave employment from doing the following within a reasonable defined period after departure:

- competing with the business in a particular geographic area
- approaching or dealing with customers with whom the employee had dealings
- using or disclosing confidential information
- poaching valuable employees.

The first two actions above can only be enforced if they are used to protect customer connections or confidential information and if they are reasonably drafted and no wider than necessary in terms of length and scope. Otherwise, they will be entirely void because they essentially prevent ex-employees from working freely (restraint of trade).

Twelve-month post-termination restrictions used to be commonplace, but it is now largely accepted that the period is too long unless the restrictions are individually justifiable.

'Garden leave' clauses can be used. Essentially, they enable an employee to be sent home during his or her notice period; the employee must not to contact customers etc. during this period and will remain subject to his or her contract of employment. This gives a breathing space for employers before restrictive covenants even bite. Such clauses are particularly useful for dealing with resigning employees. However, their use needs to be justified to protect company property in much the same way as restrictive covenants, and employees need to be paid and provided with benefits during the period of the garden leave. Also, it is extremely difficult to place a person on garden leave without an effective garden leave clause in their contract (see Section 4, page 24).

It should be remembered that it is not uncommon for architects to carry out other jobs or projects outside their main employment, and this is often seen as a tried and tested way of establishing their own reputation or practice. Flexibility by employers towards these activities can benefit employer and employee alike, but employers are still entitled to protect their own legitimate interests in their property.

### Confidentiality

Contracts commonly state that all company property (including confidential information) must be returned to an employer on demand, or in any event at the end of employment.

True trade secrets or highly confidential information belonging to an employer cannot be used by an employee or disclosed to third parties after he or she leaves employment, irrespective of what the contract says. However, it is common protection for a confidentiality clause to be drafted, in which employer and employee agree a list of confidential information that must not be disclosed to third parties or used after termination. This should include anything that the employer expressly tells an employee is confidential during employment.

Employees should also be made aware of and should comply with obligations of confidentiality owed by the employer to third parties (for example, confidentiality provisions in the RIBA *Standard Form of Agreement for the Appointment of an Architect* SFA/99).

**Intellectual property**

All businesses create and use intellectual property. Many rights are protected by law, but employees need to understand ownership and assist in taking steps to give their employers protection.

The main protections are in respect of copyright, patents, trademarks and designs.

*Copyright*

Copyright is designed to protect the expression of an idea, such as in written works or sound broadcasts (including computer software). Copyright is created automatically on creation of a work for the lifetime of the owner plus 70 years and prevents the work being copied without permission. Ownership transfers by written assignment.

*Patents*

Patents are designed to protect inventions capable of industrial application and which nobody else knows about. Patent protection is applied for at the Patent Office and gives 20 years' protection against use of the invention. The inventor applies for the patent, unless he or she is an employee acting in the course of employment. Commonly, employees still assign patent rights to employers.

*Trademarks*

Trademarks are signs, logos, etc., or other identifying factors used to distinguish products, etc., from others. They are registrable, like patents. Protection is against infringement by using identical works or where there is a likelihood of confusion.

*Designs*

Designs can be registered with the Patent Office. This gives protection against use of that or a similar design for 25 years.

## Monitoring employees

Monitoring employees by reading e-mails, monitoring calls and tracking internet use has become a complex issue. The rights revolve around whether businesses have a valid business need to monitor, and whether the employee has consented or is aware monitoring can take place. Covert (that is, undisclosed) monitoring is very difficult to justify.

Employers should have clear policies for dealing with their stated interests and outlining their methods of monitoring.

A number of areas impact on the ability of employers to monitor employees, as follows:

- The Human Rights Act 1998, which includes the right to privacy of private and family life.
- Regulation of Investigatory Powers Act 2000 (RIPA), which prevents interception of communications.
- Telecommunications (Lawful Business Practice) (Interruption of Communication) Regulations 2000, which assist businesses in intercepting to monitor or record communications relevant to the business (including reputation, standards, crime and unauthorised use of systems) and security. Employees must be made reasonably aware of the possibility of interception.
- Data Protection Act 1998, which contains certain rules relevant to the computerised monitoring of personal data or manual records and processing of data and establishes the need for transparency.
- Employment codes issued by the Information Commissioner under data protection powers, especially those relating to monitoring and the need to act proportionately (see *Checklist* and *Where to look,* below).

## Checklist

☐ **Establish the types of property your company has a genuine interest in protecting. You will need to prove that property is genuinely important in order to protect it.**

☐ Use reasonable restrictive covenants in contracts. There is no point in applying wider covenants than are reasonable.

☐ Include confidential information clauses in contracts. In any event, adapt practices so that confidential information is clearly pointed out to employees as highly confidential when it is provided.

☐ Review contracts to deal with intellectual property; ensure that it clearly covers assignment.

☐ Adopt clear policies to deal with employee monitoring.

☐ Review employment practices codes issued by the Information Commissioner to assist in reviewing business practices.

**Where to look**

**Key legislation**

Copyright, Designs and Patents Act 1988
Data Protection Act 1988
Employment Act 2002
Employment Act 2002 (Dispute Resolution) Regulations 2004
Employment Rights Act 1996
Freedom of Information Act 2000
Human Rights Act 1998
Regulation of Investigatory Powers Act 2000
Rehabilitation of Offenders Act 1974
Telecommunications (Lawful Business Practice) (Interruption of Communications) Regulations 2000

**Guidance**

*Employment Covenants and Confidential Information: law, practice and technique,* Selwyn Bloch and Kate Brearley, Butterworths Law, ISBN 0406977313

British Security Industry Association
*Information Destruction Standard*
www.bsia.co.uk

### Business Continuity Institute
*Good Practice Guidelines*
www.thebci.org

### Criminal Records Bureau
*Employing Ex-Offenders: a practical guide*
**www.crb.gov.uk**

### Home Office
*The Regulation of Investigatory Powers Act (RIPA) Codes of Practice*
www.homeoffice.gov.uk

### Information Commissioner
*Quick Guide to the Employment Practices Code: ideal for small businesses*
General guidance for private and public sector employers is available from the Information Commissioner's website
www.informationcommissioner.gov.uk

### Metropolitan Police
Fraud alert advice is available from the Metropolitan Police website
www.met.police.uk/fraudalert

### Security Industry Authority
Approved Contractor Scheme
www.the-sia.org.uk

---

**CASE STUDY**

### Facts

John is a young architect employed by Architect & Partners. He is a bright prospect, and as he develops he is exposed to key clients of the firm. Architect & Partners grows to trust him, but never quite gets round to giving him a contract of employment, or to notifying him of any of the new policies they have just finalised.

CONTINUED ▶

## CASE STUDY (CONTINUED)

After a year working for the firm one of the partners suspects that John is up to no good. He wants to monitor John's e-mails and phone calls to see what has been going on. However, the firm has no policies relating to monitoring and no actual or implied consent from John to monitor his communications.

A few days later John leaves to join a large competitor of the firm. It immediately becomes clear that he is approaching key clients of the firm and soliciting them to become clients of his new employer and that he has taken client lists and key drawings and designs with him. He also knows the charging structure of Architect & Partners and is proposing to undercut them. The firm receives advice that nothing can be done about these issues because the firm has not protected itself.

### Issues

- Although there are some implied terms relating to not competing with an employer during employment and not using trade-secret style confidential information after employment has terminated, they are difficult to prove.
- Proper monitoring policies could have helped when there was a suspicion of wrongdoing on the part of John.
- Properly drafted restrictive covenants could have provided protection against John poaching clients and joining competitors for a defined period.
- A proper 'garden leave' clause might have assisted in giving the firm a breathing space to cement relationships with clients. It would have kept John continually employed and so subject to contract terms but out of the office and so out of contact with clients.
- A clause describing true confidential information could have been utilised to protect misuse of trade information, client lists, drawings and designs during and after employment.

# Section 10
# Employment policies

*This section deals with some of the issues surrounding staff handbooks and policies, and the key distinction between contractually binding terms of employment and pure policies.*

## Issues and alarm bells

Companies often issue their staff with staff handbooks. Staff handbooks are often used to set out company ideals and mission statements and are a very convenient way of giving new employees as much information as possible about the structure and culture of an organisation.

Handbooks can incorporate some contractual terms of a contract of employment (see Section 4, page 19) or can contain pure policies (or possibly both). Care needs to be taken to ensure that policies and procedures that are designed to be non-contractual do not become contractual or confused with contractual obligations.

A format should be used that is easy to update. Intranet sites can be used when publishing the handbook, but ensure that all employees have access to a copy of the handbook. If updating by e-mail or intranet, ensure that a record of changes is kept and that there is a system for recording receipt of the updated sections.

The way that new policies are introduced should be carefully considered. Even if policies do not constitute contractual terms, it is always best practice to consult with affected staff before introducing new or changed policies. It would be prudent to adopt a flexible approach during the early stages of introduction.

The subjects covered in the contents of a handbook can vary, but the following should be considered:

- Essential:

  - disciplinary and grievance procedure
  - family-friendly policies, including maternity, paternity and adoption leave, emergency time off for dependants and parental leave
  - holiday leave and pay
  - sick leave and pay
  - equal opportunities
  - pay and benefits (including overtime pay)
  - deductions from wages (including recovery of overpayments)
  - hours of work
  - notice periods
  - health and safety policy (this could be published as a separate document or handbook)
  - information and consultation arrangements (if any)
  - collective agreements (if any).

- Optional:

  - introduction to the organisation
  - organisation chart
  - internet and e-mail policy
  - harassment and bullying
  - incapacity and capability
  - absence policy
  - performance management and appraisal
  - drugs and alcohol
  - smoking
  - training
  - dress code
  - gifts and hospitality
  - expenses procedure
  - company equipment (mobile phones, laptops, tools, etc.)
  - forms for in-house use
  - housekeeping
  - flexible working arrangements
  - reference policy
  - redundancy

- bereavement and compassionate leave
- jury service
- bank holiday working
- time off for trade union representatives (if applicable)
- whistle-blowing
- stress.

## Checklist

When establishing policies and handbooks, take the following steps:

- ☐ **Consider current employment legislation and how it affects your policies and procedures.**

- ☐ **Use bullet points, short sentences and paragraph subheadings in a crisp formal fashion.**

- ☐ **Choose a format that is easy to update (e.g. loose-leaf or ring binders) – make sure it is clear when updated sections are created and notified to staff.**

- ☐ **Think about a 'frequently asked questions' (FAQs) section.**

- ☐ **Consult managers and staff when drafting new policies and procedures.**

- ☐ **Get the contents checked from a legal perspective before publishing.**

Get all publications proofread to reduce errors or typing mistakes.

Try to avoid:

- ☐ **using long paragraphs**

- ☐ **using foreign or Latin phrases**

- ☐ **using jargon, clichés or humour**

- ☐ **vague language, which can lead to misinterpretation, resulting in disputes with your employees.**

## Where to look

### Key legislation

Copyright, Designs and Patents Act 1988
Data Protection Act 1988

Employment Act 2002
Employment Act 2002 (Dispute Resolution) Regulations 2004
Employment Relations Act 2004
Employment Rights Act 1988
Employment Rights Act 1996
Equal Pay Act 1970
Freedom of Information Act 2000
Health and Safety at Work etc. Act 1974
Management of Health and Safety at Work Regulations 1999
Public Interest Disclosure Act 1988
Working Time Regulations 1988 (as amended)
See also key legislation for Section 6 relating to discrimination.

## Guidance

### ACAS

*The A–Z of Work: advisory handbook*
www.acas.org.uk

### RIBA

*RIBA Employment Policy*
www.riba.org

### Workplace Law Network

Template policy and procedures documentation is available from the Workplace
Law Network website
www.workplacelaw.net

See also other sections of this guide for relevant information on specific policy
areas.

# Section 11
# Staff development

*This section examines an organisation's greatest asset: its people. In order for a business to succeed, everyone has to perform well. A business can gain an advantage over its competitors by having a well-trained workforce. The benefits include improved earnings, productivity and profitability, among others.*

**Issues and alarm bells**

Rapid economic change and faster depreciation of new skills have led to a greater need for employers to invest in ongoing training to ensure that employee skills are constantly updated. And there is good reason to suppose that these skills requirements will go on rising. However, employers are often criticised by government for not providing enough training, and they are increasingly reporting widespread skills shortages.

Since 1998, there have been a significant number of changes in training and development practices used in the UK. These include a shift from 'training' to 'learning'. 'Learning' is the process by which a person constructs new knowledge, skills and capabilities, whereas 'training' is one of several responses an organisation can undertake to promote learning.

There is no catch-all legislation within the UK that relates to training in the workplace, although in some areas (such as age or disability awareness) there is an expectation upon employers to provide training to meet the requirements of specific Acts or Regulations. Employers are generally expected to take a voluntary approach to the provision of training and development, which is after all in their own interests.

To ensure that architects undertake regular training and development activities (in common with other chartered institutions), the RIBA takes a mandatory approach.

The policy of Continuing Professional Development (CPD) requires architects to undertake a minimum of 35 hours (or 100 points) per year of CPD. Failure to do so can result in suspension from chartered status.

For support staff, regular training and development opportunities lead to greater competence in existing roles. In turn, this helps the business to respond to change and overcome uncertainty in trading conditions.

The benefits of some training may be perceived as intangible, for example improved motivation or customer satisfaction. As a result, it may be tempting to ignore or neglect staff development, particularly for support staff, until mistakes or problems such as poor performance or complaints become obvious.

In a similar way, the benefits of non-technical 'soft skills' training, such as communication or management skills, can be difficult to measure in terms of return on investment. As a result, there is a tendency within the architectural sector to put a higher emphasis on content or 'hard' aspects of training, such as knowledge and technical skills.

### Who should be trained?

There remains inequality in learning provision. Those with higher levels of qualifications are more likely to receive training, as are those in younger age groups. People with degrees are more confident in initiating training, and they tend to undertake more learning outside the workplace.

Those with a lower level of educational attainment tend to prefer more passive approaches, such as on-the-job training. This tends to be well received by employees, although high levels of organisational support are required.

According to a Chartered Institute of Personnel and Development (CIPD) survey conducted in March 2005, women are more likely to receive training than men, and 71 per cent of over 55s receive training. Evidence suggests that part-time employees receive marginally fewer training days (a mean average of 4.3 days compared with 5.1 days for full-time employees).

### How much training do people receive?

The mean amount of time spent on training activities during 2004 was 4.9 days per employee. Employees in small businesses are least likely to receive training from their employers. According to the CIPD's 2005 survey, employees in firms with more than 100 employees are more than twice as likely to receive training than those working in smaller organisations.

The observation that individuals who possess a degree are more likely to initiate training themselves appears to confirm that the more learning an individual under-goes, the more confident they are in requesting further opportunities. Initiation of training by individuals is more likely to occur in organisations with fewer than 20 employees, where it is unlikely that there will be a human resources (HR) or training department.

**How successful is training?**

The CIPD survey shows that 50 per cent of those undertaking training thought it had been 'very successful', while 44 per cent judged it to have been 'quite successful'. These striking results confirm the importance of training in the workplace and the value that employees put on these opportunities.

As might be expected, there is a close correlation between the size of an organisation and the likelihood of it having an HR or training department, and also whether employees have the opportunity of assessing whether their training has been successful. This is clearly an issue for owners and managers in small organisations as there is the possibility that training activities might not meet organisational objectives.

The support of line managers is essential in driving training and in evaluating its effectiveness. Getting management buy-in for training and ensuring that line managers are serious in their approach to learning remains a priority for smaller practices within the architectural sector.

**Forms of training**

The two most common forms of training are teaching in a meeting room or class-room and on-the-job training. However, research shows that coaching is a growing trend, particularly for managers.

Learners prefer active rather than passive learning. This is particularly true for those with no or low levels of qualifications, who prefer being shown something and then practising it. Being taught in a meeting room or classroom and learning from colleagues are the next most popular activities for learners.

The least popular methods of learning include reading books and articles, watching videos and correspondence courses.

**Barriers to training**

The main reasons given by people for turning down an offer of training are that they are too busy or that the training is not relevant to their job.

**Cost of training**

Being able to calculate how much an organisation spends on training and development activities is an important activity. An organisation needs to know this in order to:

- prepare training plans and budgets
- carry out assessments of whether particular training interventions provide value for money
- make decisions about whether to buy in training services or provide them in-house
- evaluate the benefits of training
- benchmark training spend against similar organisations'
- calculate the return on investment in staff training.

The type of activity will affect how easy or complicated it is to cost the training. For example, sending people on an external training course is relatively easy to cost as there will be a cost per person charged for the course plus any associated travel, accommodation and subsistence costs. More difficult is the costing of developing and delivering a course from scratch.

Whatever training activity is chosen, it is important to consider the hidden costs of employees' time away from work. This is particularly important when making assessments of value for money, and is easily overlooked.

Remember, however, that there are certain areas of your business where you cannot afford *not* to invest in training: key health and safety legislation includes a legal requirement to provide staff with sufficient information, instruction, training and supervision to enable them to work safely.

**Checklist**

☐ Link training to long-term strategic business plans. This is far more beneficial than short-term responses to market conditions.

☐ Remember to include all staff when drawing up a training and development policy.

☐ Emphasise that staff should take some responsibility for their own learning opportunities. Encourage them to highlight training needs throughout the year and ask them to suggest opportunities and ideas for learning events.

☐ Set funds aside for a dedicated annual training budget – perhaps a percentage of sales.

☐ Formally assess training needs at least once a year. A performance appraisal or skills audit is a good place to start. Having up-to-date job descriptions with person specifications will help you.

☐ Manage expectations – training doesn't automatically lead to promotion in every case, so be careful about what is promised. In most situations, it aims to help individuals to perform to the best of their ability in their current role.

☐ Training doesn't always mean formal classroom-style learning. For example:

- teaching others provides a better understanding of the subject matter
- involvement in a project team creates greater knowledge of a subject
- leading a project team provides people-management skills
- participating in contract negotiations provides legal knowledge, negotiating skills, people skills and a wider understanding of the issues
- troubleshooting provides investigative and problem-solving skills.

☐ As an employer, you are not allowed to charge your staff for any health and safety training they undertake. Remember also that you may need to have trained first-aid personnel available, not only in offices but also on any site where work is undertaken.

## Where to look

### Key legislation

Health and Safety at Work etc. Act 1974
Management of Health and Safety at Work Regulations 1999

### Guidance

*The Staff Development Handbook: an action kit to improve performance*, Peter Sheal, Kogan Page, ISBN 0749429399

### Chartered Institute of Personnel and Development

www.cipd.co.uk

### Health and Safety Executive

www.hse.gov.uk

# Section 12

# TUPE: the transfer of staff with businesses and service contracts

*This section is designed as a brief introduction to the Transfer of Undertakings (Protection of Employment) Regulations 1981 and their potential application, with some indications of potential forthcoming amendments. This is a complex subject and this section does not attempt to cover it in any detail (the* Where to look *section, below, gives further sources of information).*

**Issues and alarm bells**

The Transfer of Undertakings (Protection of Employment) Regulations 1981 (TUPE) essentially provide automatic protection to employees if their employer changes and their employment moves across to that new employer in situations where TUPE applies. TUPE was originally designed to apply only to the sale or takeover of companies, but its application has been expanded to other types of transaction.

**Basic effects of TUPE applying**

Employment automatically transfers when the employer changes; it is as if the incoming employer had always employed the transferring employee. Terms and conditions of employment transfer, as do liabilities, such as unpaid arrears of pay or pay rises agreed just prior to the transfer. Further, they cannot be changed if the reason for the change is the transfer, even if employees consent.

Transferring terms and conditions of employment do not include occupational pension schemes to the extent they operate at the end of a normal working life. However, early retirement benefits paid in the event of redundancy and benefits payable on early retirement can transfer, even if housed in a pension scheme.

Dismissals made before or after the transfer for a reason connected to it are automatically unfair and give rise to unfair dismissal liabilities passing to the incoming employer, subject to an 'eto reason' defence being available.

## Potential application

The following situations are now accepted as potentially giving rise to the application of TUPE. Companies should beware of these situations and consider the application of TUPE and whether staff carrying out work before the relevant transaction will transfer under TUPE.

- Business sales (although TUPE does not apply to share sales).
- Contracting-out of services – for example, a company ceasing to carry out its own in-house catering and instead contracting-out catering to a third party contractor (Contractor A). In such circumstances the company employees who performed the in-house catering could transfer to Contractor A with the protection of TUPE.
- Reassignment of services – for example, where the contract of Contractor A is ended and a new contract to provide the catering service activities is won by Contractor B. In those circumstances, Contractor B could inherit the staff of Contractor A.
- In-sourcing – for example, where the company decides to take the catering services back in-house from Contractor B.
- Leases – TUPE can apply where a business lease is surrendered or forfeited and a new lease is granted to run the same business. Employees involved in the business can transfer from the outgoing tenant to the incoming tenant under the protection of TUPE.

## Public authority TUPE transactions

The questions of whether TUPE has in recent times held less importance in relation to many public-sector contracting-out situations is due to the practice of insistence by the public sector that private-sector contractors must agree in a contract that TUPE is deemed to apply in practice at commencement and termination of the contract irrespective of the actual legal position. Further, in National Health Service (NHS) outsourcing situations, the NHS Retention of Employment model has taken a bolder stance in relation to the soft facilities management 'five trades' (portering, catering, domestics, laundry and custody and security services). This attempts to prevent TUPE from applying due to employees electing not to transfer from NHS employment and secondment agreements being entered into with the contractor.

### New TUPE regulations

In September 2001 the Government produced a long-awaited public consultation document setting out its proposals for the reform of the TUPE regulations. A significant number of questions were posed in the document.

New TUPE regulations were to be produced by October 1992 but have been much delayed. In March 2005 the Government produced a consultation document setting out its proposals on drafting for new TUPE regulations to give effect to its stated aims to amend TUPE (see www.dti.gov.uk/er). The potential implementation of new regulations was delayed until April 2006, but it is likely that the new regulations will include provision for:

- TUPE to apply to most changes or service provision contracts
- some assistance to make transfer-related changes to terms of employment easier
- some duties for an outgoing employer to provide information about the transferring employees to incoming employers
- assistance to soften the effect of TUPE in certain insolvency situations where there is a 'rescue culture' designed to save the business.

### Checklist

☐ **Be aware of the potential application of TUPE; it can arise in unexpected situations.**

☐ **Any merger, takeover or acquisition will attract the application of TUPE, unless it is made by share sale (TUPE does not apply to share sales).**

☐ **Take extra care if tendering for outsourced service contracts. If a workforce employed by a third party, or part of it, is currently performing the work, there is a risk that they could transfer under TUPE.**

☐ **If a potential TUPE situation arises it is prudent to enter into a clear agreement with the current employer, if possible, as to the agreed application of TUPE, making provisions for splitting up responsibility for the relevant** staff before and after the transaction and clarifying the responsibilities for any envisaged dismissals.

**Where to look**

### Key legislation

Acquired Rights Directive 2001 (2001/23/EC)
Transfer of Undertakings (Protection of Employment) Regulations 1981

### Guidance

*Tolley's Employment Handbook*, 18th edition, Tolley Publishing, ISBN 0754527077

### ACAS

*Employment Rights on the Transfer of an Undertaking*
*Employee Communications and Consultation: advisory booklet*
*Redundancy Handling: advisory booklet*
www.acas.org.uk

### Department of Trade and Industry

*Transfers of Undertakings: a guide to the regulations*
www.dti.gov.uk

---

**CASE STUDY**

#### Facts

Architect & Partners has grown to a reasonable size. It has a good flow of work, but a relatively small niche firm of local architects, Small Co., which has a strong reputation for drawing work, is starting to compete. Architect & Partners resolves to ask that firm to merge with it.

Negotiations progress and it is decided that a takeover will take place on 30 April. Architect & Partners proposes to purchase the business of Small Co. in its entirety. On 29 April, Small Co. dismisses two employees that Architect & Partners says it does not want. In addition, after the takeover has been completed, all of the Small Co. employees say that they have outstanding unpaid bonuses from last year and another bonus has just become due.

CONTINUED ▶

CASE STUDY (CONTINUED)

### Issues

- TUPE would apply to this takeover; the Small Co. employees would be protected by TUPE.
- The 'transfer' would take place on the takeover date of 30 April.
- If the two employees dismissed on 29 April brought claims of unfair dismissal, it is likely that they would be successful on the basis that the dismissals were made because of the transfer; the dismissals could therefore be deemed automatically unfair.
- Even though Small Co. dismissed the two employees on 29 April, before the transfer, the liability for the unfair dismissal would rest with Architect & Partners as it would transfer to them under TUPE.
- If the Small Co. employees could show that the bonuses were contractual terms of their employment, liability to pay them would transfer to Architect & Partners under TUPE. Moreover, the bonus could not be changed or removed as a term of employment if the reason for the change was connected to the transfer taking place.
- A properly constructed sale and purchase agreement could have dealt with these issues and set out an agreement to split the liabilities between Small Co. and Architect & Partners, rather than all the liability resting with Architect & Partners.

# Section 13
# Discipline and termination

*This section deals with issues arising towards the end of employment: termination, dismissal and references. It also deals with practices surrounding discipline and grievances, and some points to watch when settling disputes and claims. Employers should note the key importance of the new statutory minimum disciplinary and dismissal procedures and their application to all disciplinary, grievance and dismissal issues.*

**Issues and alarm bells**

Issues of disciplinary action and termination of employment can be very complex and are areas to be approached with caution. Various useful sources of guidance produced by ACAS and the Department of Trade and Industry (DTI) cover most of the issues (see *Where to look*, below).

The basic issues set out in this section flag the areas that need to be thought about before disciplinary action, dismissal or termination of employment is considered.

**Termination of employment**

Termination of employment can take place in a number of ways. Note that not all terminations constitute a 'dismissal'. Dismissals give employees specific rights.

Typically, termination of employment will occur in one of the following ways:

- dismissal by employer – with or without notice
- resignation by an employee – this is not usually a 'dismissal'
- expiry and non-renewal of a fixed-term contract – this is a 'dismissal'
- constructive dismissal – where an employee resigns as a result of a fundamental breach of contract by his or her employer; in essence this makes a resignation into a 'dismissal'
- frustration – where the contract becomes impossible to perform (quite rare, usually due to sickness or imprisonment); this is not a dismissal.

It should be noted in particular that the new statutory minimum disciplinary and dismissal procedures must now be followed for most dismissals, and that these include the ending of fixed-term contracts and compulsory retirement.

## Dismissals

True dismissals give employees a number of rights; typically potential claims for breach of contract and rights to claim 'unfair dismissal' (see below).

Unless an employee is guilty of gross misconduct, he or she has a right to receive notice (either the amount of notice in the contract, or if it is silent the right to receive 'reasonable notice'). The minimum amount of notice to be given to an employee is as follows:

- one week's notice to an employee with over 1 month but less than two years of service
- one week's notice for each full year of service to an employee with over two years but under 12 years of service
- 12 weeks' notice to an employee with 12 or more years of service.

Contractual notice is often longer than minimum notice. If a contract is silent as to notice, reasonable notice is due (based on the status of the employee and industry or employer norms).

Failure to pay notice can lead to a claim for damages equivalent to salary and benefits that would have fallen due in the notice period.

## Unfair dismissal

Unfair dismissal damages claims can be expensive for employers. Avoidance of claims is a matter of the employer having a valid reason for dismissal and following a proper procedure (usually including consultation with the employee) before any decision to dismiss is taken, to make the ultimate dismissal reasonable and fair.

Usually, employees need to have one year's continuous service to qualify to claim unfair dismissal. However, if the reason for dismissal is proven to be one of a number of specific reasons, the dismissal will be 'automatically unfair'; some of the most important are:

- health and safety dismissals
- pregnancy or maternity dismissals

- dismissals for reporting protected disclosures ('whistle-blowing', see Section 6, page 40)
- dismissals connected to TUPE transfers (see Section 12, page 80).

(The guidance listed in *Where to look*, below, gives full details.)

There are only a few potentially fair reasons for a dismissal, as follows:

- Lack of capability to do the job – this involves lack of skill, qualifications, poor performance or illness.
- Misconduct – significant misconduct justifying dismissal.
- Redundancy – this has a specific definition, involving a dismissal where:

  - the employer ceases to carry on business in the place where the employee is employed, or
  - the employer's requirements for employees to carry out work of a particular kind has ceased or diminished or is expected to do so. In basic terms this means there is no or less need for employees to carry out a particular type of work.

- Breach of legislation – where a piece of legislation would be breached if the employee were to continue to work (e.g. a driver losing his or her driving licence).
- Some other substantial reason – this has been used to justify a number of business-related reasons, such as reorganisations and dismissals of employees who refuse to accept justifiable changes to terms of employment.

**Fairness and procedures**

Different potentially fair procedures apply to different reasons for dismissal. Ultimately, the question is whether the employer has acted reasonably in all the circumstances.

In determining what is reasonable a tribunal will assess the size and administrative resources of the employer. The bigger the employer, the more is expected of them. However, this does not mean that small employers do not need to follow fair procedures.

See *Where to look*, below, for sources of detailed guidance as to the appropriate processes. A few typical procedures for different types of dismissals are as follows:

- Conduct: carry out a full investigation; inform the employee of the allegations and the evidence; hold a hearing at which the employee can put his or her case and be accompanied; apply the appropriate penalty if there are reasonable grounds to believe the employee is guilty.

- Capability: inform the employee why his or her performance is poor; state what must improve and how quickly improvement must occur; hold a meeting at each stage of the process at which the employee can state his or her case and be accompanied; before any decision is taken to give a warning or to dismiss, consider training to assist the employee and whether alternative jobs are available internally that would better suit the employee.
- Sickness: get a medical prognosis; consult fully with the employee; in certain circumstances employers may be able to dismiss if it is not reasonable to wait for a lengthy recovery. The key is to understand the true reason for sickness. Note the crossover with the Disability Discrimination Act (see Section 6, page 34).
- Redundancy: give as much warning as possible of a potential redundancy position; establish objectively fair selection criteria for selecting staff for potential redundancy; consider and consult in relation to suitable alternative posts; consult fully with staff before any final decision is taken to dismiss for redundancy. (Note that if over 20 redundancies are proposed in any 90-day period, special collective consultation rules apply and it will be necessary to consult with trade unions or elected employee representatives and to notify the DTI.)
- Some other substantial reason: there is no set procedure, but it will always be necessary to consult with employees and to consider alternative employment.

### Minimum disciplinary, dismissal and grievance procedures

Note that since October 2004 the Employment Act 2002 (Dispute Resolution) Regulations 2004 mean that any dismissal can be unfair unless a minimum process is followed. The minimum process must involve at least a letter informing the employee of the potential dismissal, a meeting at which he or she can be accompanied by a trade union official or a fellow employee and at which the employee is given the full chance to state his or her case and a right of appeal. This is necessary before the types of dismissal listed above as well as expiry of fixed-term contracts and retirement. Failure by employers to follow the minimum procedures can lead to damages being increased by up to 50 per cent.

The minimum procedures do not apply to mere warnings (verbal or written). However, see *Where to look*, below, for details of guidance on disciplinary action and warnings (especially ACAS guidance). Proper procedures should nonetheless be followed before verbal or written warnings are given.

Employers should have written grievance procedures for employees to follow if they wish to complain about treatment afforded to them by employers. Typically, this will involve the right to complain to a manager who has not previously been involved with the issues.

The statutory minimum procedures set out a minimum grievance procedure. This involves at least:

- the need for the grievance to be in writing (Step 1)
- the right to attend a meeting with a right to be accompanied (Step 2)
- a right of appeal against the decision (Step 3).

Various bars exist to issuing employment tribunal proceedings if employees do not follow the minimum grievance procedures in an effort to resolve the matter internally first.

### References

References can be dangerous for employers; numerous liabilities attach to the giving of a reference. There is no duty on an architect employer to give a reference unless a contract says a reference must be given.

If compiling a reference, distinct duties are owed:

- to use reasonable skill and care in compiling the reference
- not to compile a reference negligently
- not to create a misleading reference
- to provide a true, accurate and fair reference
- disciplinary action should only be referred to if the employee is aware of the action or allegations and a full investigation has already been carried out following which the employer has reasonable grounds to believe that the allegations are true.

References given as part of a settlement agreement must be given carefully; they are nonetheless references and the above rules apply. Resist the temptation to make them more 'rosy' as part of a settlement.

### Disputes and settlements

Employees typically bring breach of contract or unfair dismissal claims in an employment tribunal. Unfair dismissal claims are subject to a statutory cap for 'basic' and 'compensatory' awards.

For the most part, claims brought in the employment tribunal must be brought within three months of the act complained of, or if the issue is about termination of employment, within three months of termination. The employer receives form ET1 from the tribunal, setting out the employee's claim, and has, for the most part, 28 days to respond.

Usually there are no costs awards in tribunals (unlike in county courts or the High Court) so the employer and employee bear their own costs, although in certain circumstances there is power to award costs of up to £10,000, wasted costs orders and preparation time orders. ACAS (the Advisory, Conciliation and Arbitration Service) is always allocated to tribunal claims, and indeed there is now a duty for ACAS to conciliate in certain conciliation periods early in the life of cases.

Settlements are commonly made out of court or before proceedings are issued. The use of 'compromise agreements', in which employees give up rights to bring specific employment claims against their employers, is commonplace. However, such agreements must follow a specific format in order to be valid, and the employer must receive advice from a qualified relevant advisor.

Employers commonly consider that they can discuss 'deals' with employees on a 'without prejudice' basis, and that such a conversation cannot be referred to later in court proceedings. To a certain extent this is true, but recent cases provide a warning that not all such conversations are truly 'without prejudice'. The parties need to understand clearly that the conversation is to be without prejudice, and the conversation must take place to settle an ongoing dispute. The fact that an employee has ongoing disciplinary or grievance proceedings is not in itself a dispute.

### Retirement

Employees and employers commonly agree in employment contracts when the retirement age of the employee will be. This is usually also the accepted normal retirement age of the company. It should be the same for male and female employees to avoid discrimination claims.

Employees above the normal retirement age of a company normally cannot bring unfair dismissal or redundancy payment claims. However, this is due to change in 2006 with the introduction of age discrimination legislation (see Section 6, page 39).

As stated above, the statutory minimum disciplinary and dismissal procedures apply to compulsory retirement situations.

**Checklist**

☐ Review employment contracts to ensure notice and dismissal clauses are clear and unambiguous.

☐ Beware the dangers of unfair dismissal claims. Always think:

- Have we got a fair reason to dismiss?
- Have we planned and followed a fair procedure?
- Have we considered alternatives to discipline or dismissal?

☐ Always consider carefully why you propose to dismiss an employee. Different procedures are necessary to deal with different reasons. Never take or record a final decision to discipline or dismiss an employee until after a fair procedure has been followed and concluded.

☐ Understand the statutory minimum disciplinary, dismissal and grievance procedures. Ideally, your written procedures should exceed these so that they can be followed and comply with the minimum at the same time.

☐ Employment contracts and procedures should make disciplinary and grievance procedures clear to employees and should clearly show how to bring a grievance.

☐ Take great care before giving references for employees. Consider the duties imposed on employers in compiling and releasing references.

☐ Understanding the potential claims employees can bring is the best place to start in taking management steps to avoid them arising.

☐ In considering settling potential claims, do not assume that all 'without prejudice' discussions are truly without prejudice. Test the position beforehand to ensure that communications will be without prejudice.

**Where to look**

**Key legislation**

Employment Act 2002
Employment Act 2002 (Dispute Resolution) Regulations 2004
Employment Relations Act 2004
Employment Rights Act 1996

Trade Union and Labour Relations (Consolidation) Act 1992

## Guidance

## ACAS
*The ACAS Arbitration Scheme for the Resolution of Unfair Dismissal Disputes (England and Wales)*
*The ACAS Arbitration Scheme for the Resolution of Unfair Dismissal Disputes (Scotland)*
*Dealing with Grievances: guide for small firms*
*Discipline and Grievance at Work: advisory handbook*
*Disciplinary and Grievance Procedures: code of practice*
*Disciplinary and Grievance Procedures Folder – six easy to follow charts to guide you through disciplinary and grievance procedures*
*Discipline and Grievances at Work: guide for small firms*
*Heading for Tribunal? The ACAS Arbitration Scheme*
*Lay-offs and Short-time Working: advisory leaflet*
*Redundancy Handling: advisory booklet*
www.acas.org.uk

## Centre for Effective Dispute Resolution
*CEDR Model Settlement Agreement*
A number of model policies and guides are available from the CEDR website
www.cedr.co.uk

## Department of Trade and Industry
*Disciplinary, Dismissal and Grievance Procedures – guidance for employers*
*Dismissal – Fair and Unfair: a guide for employers*
*Redundancy Consultation and Notification*
www.dti.gov.uk

## Employment Appeals Tribunal
www.employmentappeals.gov.uk

## Employment Tribunals Online
www.employmenttribunals.gov.uk

---

**CASE STUDY**

### Facts

Architect & Partners has recently changed its emphasis and is planning to move towards focusing on providing services to the public sector rather than the private sector. The firm has secured a number of contracts for the future, and takes the view that there are areas of the business in which it can reorganise its structure to reduce overheads and to set itself up to be better able to meet client expectations for the future.

One of the products of this thinking is that the firm feels it no longer needs a director of marketing. It is thought that it can manage with one junior marketing assistant and will outsource any other work to a consultant. As a result, the role of marketing director will be redundant.

The senior partner holds a meeting with the marketing director. In the meeting, he tells her of the plans for reorganisation but that no final decisions have been taken. He also warns her that her position could, as a result, become redundant but that a period of consultation would commence and take place before any final decisions were taken. He also tells her that during the consultation period she can raise any issues that may affect any final decision to make her position redundant, and that the firm will look for suitable alternative work for her and consult with her in relation to the alternative work position. A letter is sent to her confirming all these points in writing.

The marketing director complains that the senior partner has already made his mind up and she thinks consultation is pointless. Nonetheless, she is continuously offered meetings to consult with her, and details of some potential alternative jobs are sent to her, which she rejects.

Near the end of the consultation period, the senior partner sends her a letter stating that before a final decision is taken as to whether to terminate her employment by reason of redundancy she is invited to a meeting to discuss the issues, at which she can be accompanied by a fellow employee or trade union official. She attends that meeting but still says that she thinks

CONTINUED ▶

---

the senior partner had already made his mind up to dismiss her before any consultation took place. The decision is taken to terminate her employment by reason of redundancy, but she is given a right of appeal.

She leaves and brings a tribunal claim for unfair dismissal, and sex discrimination, alleging that she was only selected for redundancy because she was female.

The tribunal decides that, taking account of all the circumstances, the dismissal was fair, and that the statutory minimum dismissal and disciplinary procedures had been complied with. They also find that the reason for the dismissal was redundancy and that the employee had not been dismissed or detrimentally treated on grounds of her gender.

### Issues

- Employers should always be careful to plan a fair process in advance. There are many pitfalls for the unwary, which can lead to findings of unfair dismissal.
- In this situation a reasonable process was followed, but it was arguably not perfect. However, each case will be judged on its merits.
- The interaction between a fair redundancy process and the statutory minimum disciplinary and dismissal procedures is unclear. However, it is essential to offer a statutory minimum dismissal procedure during a redundancy process before final decisions are taken to dismiss.
- Note that one of the key issues in this case would have been that the senior partner initially presented the position as a warning of a potential restructuring and a potential redundancy prior to consultation, rather than presenting decisions that had already been made.
- Recording meetings in writing assists in proving intentions and discussions at a later date.
- Setting out the business rationale for the reorganisation would have assisted in defending the sex discrimination claim.

# Appendix
# Sources of further information

The following list of sources of information is by no means comprehensive. However, in combination with the information in this guide, it should provide you with a useful starting point for taking specific issues further.

Government websites have improved vastly in the past two years and most now provide an extremely useful service, offering searchable information free of charge online or in the form of downloadable documentation. For example, much information that previously had to be purchased in book format is now freely – and instantly – available in Adobe Acrobat pdf format.

UK-based members of the RIBA enjoy limited free access to the information available through the Workplace Law Network's online service at www.workplacelaw.net/riba

Advisory, Conciliation and Arbitration
    Service (ACAS)
01909 533196
www.acas.org.uk

British Security Industry Association
    (BSIA)
01905 21464
www.bsia.co.uk

Business Continuity Institute
0870 603 8783
www.thebci.org

Commission for Architecture and the
    Built Environment (CABE)
020 7960 2400
www.cabe.org.uk

Centre for Effective Dispute Resolution
020 7536 6000
www.cedr.co.uk

Chartered Institute of Personnel and
    Development (CIPD)
020 8971 9000
www.cipd.co.uk

Commission for Racial Equality
020 7939 000
www.cre.gov.uk

Department for Work and Pensions
020 7712 2171
www.dwp.gov.uk

Department of Health
020 7210 4850
www.dh.gov.uk

Department of Trade and Industry
020 7215 5000
www.dti.gov.uk

Disability Rights Commission
08457 622 633
www.drc-gb.org

Employment Appeals Tribunal
020 7273 1041
www.employmentappeals.co.uk

Employment Lawyers Association
01895 256972
www.elaweb.org.uk

Employment Tribunal
0845 795 9775
www.employmenttribunals.gov.uk

Equal Opportunities Commission
0845 601 5901
www.eoc.org.uk

Financial Services Authority
020 7066 1000
www.fsa.gov.uk

Health and Safety Executive
08701 545 500
www.hse.gov.uk

HM Revenue and Customs
08457 143 143
www.hmrc.gov.uk

Home Office
0870 000 1585
www.homeoffice.gov.uk

Information Commissioner's Office
01625 545 700
www.informationcommissioner.gov.uk

Investors in People
020 7467 1900
www.iipuk.co.uk

Kennedys Solicitors
020 7638 3688
www.kennedys-law.com

Office of the Deputy Prime Minsister
020 7709 9808
www.odpm.gov.uk

Public Concern at Work
020 7404 6609
www.pcaw.co.uk

RIBA Bookshops
020 7496 8390
www.ribabookshops.com

Royal Institute of British Architects (RIBA)
020 7580 5533
www.architecture.com

Security Industry Authority (SIA)
08702 430 100
www.the-sia.org.uk

Tailored Interactive Guidance on
        Employment Rights (TIGER)
www.tiger.gov.uk

Trades Union Congress (TUC)
020 7636 4030
www.tuc.org.uk

Work Foundation
0870 165 6700
www.theworkfoundation.com

Workplace Law Group
0870 777 8881
www.workplacelaw.net

# Index